The Next Maverick

READY TO SHAPE THE FUTURE

AJI R. MICHAEL

Published by:
The Vine Media Communications Ltd
Web: www.thevinemedia.co.uk

On behalf of:
Head Affairs Publishing
A division of Head Affairs Coaching Ltd
Designing Solutions with Leaders in MindTM
Web: www.headaffairs.com

Design & Print: www.TheVineMedia.co.uk

ISBN978-0-9575765-4-4
Printed in the United Kingdom

ACKNOWLEDGEMENTS

I would like to thank my friends and families who gave generously of their time and wisdom via e-mail, phone as well as face to face.

Additionally, I thank my brother Moses, the best business partner anyone could wish for. His support and guidance are beyond words themselves. I do hope you remember my text message where I said "Done is better than Perfect".

Most of all, I thank my husband Michael. His steadfast love, support and guidance changed my life. Thank you for taking time out to go through my work, correcting my grammar, asking for clarifications and giving me the confidence that the work is good to go.

Above all, I appreciate the Holy Spirit without whose partnership none of this would have been possible.

PREFACE

"The man who grasps principles can successfully select his own methods.
The man who tries methods, ignoring principles, is sure to have trouble."

\- Ralph Waldo Emerson

L ike any entrepreneur, I have a fascination with success. I love reading stories of successful entrepreneurs, especially those who change the way the various industries operate. When I read these stories, I ponder on how they happened. I ask myself numerous questions, for instance, What are those things they did or do which enabled them to get the grip to be exceptional? Some of them may seem obvious until you consider the multifaceted processes they have to put together to maintain high rates of successful business enterprises. I figured out it is not luck nor coincidences but rather, something more than these two are involved. Although luck or coincidences do occur, they do not provide a sustainable successful future.

Since you are reading this book, there is no doubt you desire to be successful as well as influence the world in some way. So the question is, how do you do it? I have no doubt that the answer is "Be different from the crowd." This book introduces twelve invaluable distinctive laws that I believe will enable any individual to become one of the most influential persons in the world- irrespective of your chosen career. Some aspects of this book such as the emphasis on value and faith, I learnt from my father. He exemplified much of what is central to us as a family: the value of hard work, integrity, humility and a lifelong dedication to learning. The most important source of research, however, was down to my own reading and study. Shortly after I became a Christian, I developed two strong passions. The first was to build a functional library. The second was to identify and understand the principles that lead to prosperity and societal growth. I always look for an opportunity to serve and help humanity. During my research, I concluded that the two passions are intimately related.

As a science student, I understood the natural world operated according to fixed laws. Through my research, I came to realise that there were, likewise, laws that govern human beings and prosperity. It seemed to me that these laws are fundamental not only to the well-being of societies, but also to the tiny communities of businesses. Indeed, that is what I discovered when I began to apply the laws systematically to my personal life. I have stumbled, succeeded and continued to grow and change. My values and conducts have evolved, and I expect them to continue to do so in the future.

My own journey as an entrepreneur was more of a roller coaster ride than a smooth drive down a freeway. I have delved into various businesses in the past. In some of these businesses, I achieved a 40% increase in profit over 3 years. In some years it was over 100% and in others it was negative 40%. One of the things I now recognise is that I had no structure against which to measure or manage success, despite being very well qualified academically in business. Yes, I had business plans, strategic plans and so forth but they were based on where I saw the opportunities or threats. What I did not see was the whole picture - I did not see how my day to day activities were connected to the whole universe. As they say, 'If only I knew then what I know now!'. On reflection I recognise that few entrepreneurs are successful by chance. You have to engineer success into your personal life, your business and by having an intimate understanding of what drives success as well as how to manage and multiply it.

From my research and my many conversations with successful entrepreneurs and exceptional individuals, I have a much better view of how success occurs and what you have to do to sustain it. In addition to that, I have been fortunate to sit in on many meetings with highly distinguished professionals and entrepreneurs and have had the opportunity of evaluating many independent contractors and businesses. It is obvious from those experiences that the 12 laws outlined in this book are invaluable and have allowed me to identify success obstacles and opportunities in business and the world at large.

In writing 'The Next Maverick', I have had two audiences in mind. The first group is the broad professionals. The book is intended to help them develop the rare traits of that exceptional employee who is sought after by employers, regardless of industry. The second audience I have in mind is broader and consists of business readers in particular, entrepreneurs. 'The Next Maverick' is not just another list of qualities of a successful entrepreneurs so common in today's management literature. It is a path for entrepreneurs to create a harmony of interest with society. For any entrepreneur to survive and prosper, he/she must create real long-term value in society and see them through. I believe nothing less than the application of all of the known universal laws can help in most instances.

These laws certainly has worked well for many exceptional and successful entrepreneurs, and there is no reason why it cannot also work well for you. Perhaps you are already successful but past performance does not guarantee future success. To continue to achieve superior results, we must continually improve our understanding and application of the 12 laws. I learned that the entrepreneurial journey is an experimental discovery toward an unknown future of increasing societal prosperity. 'The Next Maverick' is on a journey of a never-ending process of learning and improvement.

To all readers of this book who endeavour to understand and apply these laws, I wish you every success on this journey as we shape the future.

CONTENTS

"What I know for sure is that if you want to have success, you can't make success your goal. The key is not to worry about being successful but to instead work towards being significant – and the success will naturally follow."
-Oprah Winfrey.

INTRODUCTION
The Next Maverick

"He that would know what shall be, must consider what hath been."

- H. G. Bohn

Sir Ian Terence Botham, OBE commented in a recent interview by the Express newspaper (Tuesday, July 16, 2013) that all he thinks about is being number one, being the best at what he does. He said "if I was a bus driver I'd want to be the best bus driver, if I was a barman I'd want to be the best barman. If you have that mentality and drive yourself on, then hopefully you will succeed." There is definitely no doubt that he did succeed. Being a former England Test cricketer and Test team captain, Botham holds a number of Test records as an all-rounder, including being the fastest (in terms of matches) to achieve the "doubles" of 1,000 runs and 100 wickets, 2,000 runs and 200 wickets, and 3,000 runs and 300 wickets. He, at one point, held the world record for the greatest number of Test wickets and still holds the record for the highest number of Test wickets taken by an England player (ESPN cricinfo). Also a prolific fundraiser for charitable causes, his efforts have raised more than £12 million for charity, with Leukaemia Research.

The Ian Botham example shows how an individual can be determined to be exceptional in their chosen career. It is no wonder that David Brent (BBC) described him as "someone who is a maverick." Right from his early age he was always single-minded. When informed that Botham wanted to be a sportsman, the Careers Mistress at his school said to him, "Fine, everyone wants to play sport, but what are you really going to do?" (Interview by BBC Radio 4's Fiona

Glover, 20 November 2010, *Saturday Live*). But Botham is not everyone; he is simply the maverick of his time.

As you would expect, successful entrepreneurs have a lot in common. Success to them is a deliberate intention. While wining can occur by chance, waiting around for it to happen is hardly a way of life for mavericks. It is not enough having a good product or service. Being an exceptional entrepreneur is a bit like a jigsaw puzzle: All the bits have to be in place before you can make it work properly. Any missing piece will ultimately create the seeds of failure. Basically, success happens by setting out to create a life and business which satisfies a number of key laws.

If I ask you, is there really one single map on the road to success? Your answer is as good as mine, you would definitely want to get hold of one of those maps, right? Most of the time people are looking for a 'one size fits all' and there isn't such a thing. There are universal laws which, if applied, can give you what you want. Assuming there is such a thing, how do you find this map? Just like a typical road, one road may cross paths with another or some may just lead to so many twists and turns. The roads to success are not one and the same. You create your own history. You create your own destiny. Following your own chart after all means you are being yourself. So how do you find the starting place and set pointers along the way?

If you would agree with me, we live in a universe that

functions by laws; predictable, repeatable and understandable laws. A Law is the highest-level science can achieve, below Laws are Theories and Hypotheses. To remind ourselves, a 'law' is defined as a statement of an order or relation of phenomena that, so far as is known, is invariable under the given conditions. While theory is defined as a plausible or scientifically acceptable general principle or body of principles offered to explain phenomena'. That means if the truth of a statement is verified repeatedly in a reproductive way then it can reach the level of a natural law. And we understand that everything we observe in the universe operates according to known natural laws.

The brain of this book is centred around the profound and powerful law that has been referred to as the "Iron Law of Human Destiny". This is none other than the Law of Cause & Effect. The Law of Cause & Effect states that absolutely everything happens for a reason. All actions have consequences and produce specific results, as do all inactions. The choices we make are causes, whether they are conscious or unconscious, and will produce corresponding outcomes or effects. The Law works the same for everyone at all times.

"Shallow men believe in luck or in circumstance. Strong men believe in cause and effect."
- Ralph Waldo Emerson

The law can be applied in the physical sense through examination of Sir Isaac Newton's third Law of Motion, which states that "for every action, there is an equal and opposite reaction." If, for example, you were to stand bare feet on a hot plate (the cause) the effect would be that your feet would burn and it would hurt! While this is an extreme example, its purpose is to illustrate the law very well.

Let us consider another situation which is specific to business. Let us assume you have received a large order that exceeds your current production staff capacity and you have a deadline to supply whilst still coping with the day to day activities. At this point, you have a choice to make – muddle through with the existing situation or hire more interim staff. Of course if hiring is your option then you will have to consider your cash flow and other recruitment factors. Whichever decision you make becomes the cause – either you hire or you don't. The effect is the result of the decision. If you hired someone, there should be some relief for your existing staff, and customers should become happier with your service (providing of course, you hired the right person or invested to train the hired staff properly). If the decision was not to hire, the effect would likely be dissatisfied, and eventually, lost customers and potentially lost employees as well – unless you can find another solution (cause) to implement (process, re-engineering etc.). This is a recipe for disaster which could easily see the business fail altogether – the ultimate effect.

The purpose of this book is also to show the interconnectedness of these laws. A major deficiency in any one attribute will ultimately have a negative impact on the individual, the business and the community. With these essential drivers in mind, the entrepreneur can examine his or her business, starting from themselves and reviewing things to see which elements need work. Being forewarned of a potential problem is a great place to start. While everything can't be fixed overnight, a plan can be put into place to work on the least desirable features of your business.

For many entrepreneurs, it is the insight they achieve through seeing this type of concept which opens their eyes to new possibilities. Often they are simply too close to their business to see the missing bits of the puzzle. Sometimes just by being taken on the journey is sufficient for them to come up with the ideas necessary to substantially improve their businesses. 'The Next Maverick' will certainly do that for many potential and exceptional entrepreneurs as well as professionals.

What can you do now:

There are three action exercises which you can put in place immediately :

1. **Establish** the key areas in which you want improvement or success. Identify the specific things you will need to do in order to get the results that you desire.

2. **Take action!** Make the decision to focus on, and do, the things that other successful people have done in those areas. Half the battle is taking action. It is your ability to actually begin that will set you apart from the majority of the population.

3. **Persevere.** If you take action and do the things that others have done, you will eventually get the desired results. Rome was not built in a day, as they say, and it has taken you a lifetime to get into the position in which you now find yourself. Success takes time, so if it doesn't seem to be working immediately, don't give up! Stay focused, analyse your causes to ensure you are doing the right things; tweak your approach if necessary – you will get the desired results!

There is no mystery to achieving success - it is available to all of us. One needs only be aware of, understand and live in accordance with these laws. In the end it may come down to personal aspirations. The entrepreneur who has the desire, energy and natural entrepreneurial ability can take this review and use it to drive change. Out of those changes will come opportunities and those may well lead to the changes in the business which move it to a situation which has greater probability of success and growth. You never know- you might just be the next maverick!

CHAPTER ONE

THE LAW OF REFLECTION

"As a man thinks in his heart, so shall he be"

– The bible

Born into poverty to a teenage single mother on welfare, she experienced considerable hardship during her childhood, raped at age nine, became pregnant at 14 and lost her child at infancy. Her sister died of causes related to cocaine addiction, her brother also died of AIDS related causes but Oprah Winfrey later became a millionaire at age 25. According to Forbes magazine, Oprah was the richest African American of the 20th century and the world's only Black billionaire for three years running. Life magazine hailed her as the most influential woman of her generation. In 2005, Business Week named her the greatest Black philanthropist in American history. Her Angel Network has raised more than $51,000,000 for charitable programs, including girls' education in South Africa and relief to the victims of Hurricane Katrina.

Has it ever occurred to you how people transition from one extreme situation to the other? Oprah is definitely not the only woman nor will she be the last who had a dysfunctional background. We have countless of them, it is not respective of any gender nor location. These are circumstances that we find ourselves as a result of our birth and upbringing. Some people might even come from a wealthy home, but still suffer abuse or addiction of different sorts. The outcome in most cases is suicide. The victims always feel that was their only option – the other extreme. As a business coach, I have had situations where after working with clients and it seems results are slow and we are not getting a headway, I always took it personal but in the end I discovered they did not actually need a business coach. Their issues were usually deeper, so much so that only a spiritualist, psychologist, or therapist could help. As an entrepreneur, I know that people, situations or events in our past always influence the decisions or choices we make.

The subconscious mind is like a video camera that is attached to us and operates 24/7. It never sleeps, it is always on duty. It has the capacity to record in three forms: Firstly, the actual event – that is you are able to recall a conversation word for word, even after several years. It also records the emotional component of the event, that is, it records how you feel about this event when it happened to you. So if the event is positive, such as a happy event, then the recording would be a positive energetic one. If however, it was negative, such as an abuse, or being abandoned, for example, then the recording would be negative. Here you think to yourself that "I am not lovable", or " they don't like me", or "I am not wanted", etc. These would be your negative reflections that you take on about yourself. The third is the perceptual component of the event, which is described as the mental body. It records how you perceive the event, which is totally different to the actual event. So if the actual event is positive, such as a happy event, then the recording would be a positive energetic one. If however it was negative, such as an abuse or a rejection, then the recording would be negative or you could have taken on a negative reflection about yourself, such as 'I can't be good enough'; 'if they loved me they would not do this to me, therefore I can't be lovable'; 'I can't trust life'; 'I have to do something for others to get something'; 'It is what they want that is important, not what I want', etc, etc.

"Without deep reflection one knows from daily life that one exists for other people"
-Albert Einstein

It is important to understand that the recordings of these events do not happen in our brains as some would like us to believe. They are recorded in our various auric bodies (an electromagnetic field around the body that protects and guides you) surrounding the body namely the etheric, emotional and mental bodies. The Auric Body connects to the Pineal gland (bringing intelligence) and corresponds to the immune system (bringing health). Now these bodies are populated by these positive and negative events that have positive and negative charges to them. It then follows that each of us are therefore electrical magnetic beings. This is the mechanism that then operates in our lives and attracts to us the events and situations in our lives being partners, opportunities, work environment, family environment, etc.

What tends to happen is that these negative events have a particular resonance to them and they wait for an opportunity in your life to arise, to come up, for us to face them and resolve them. Our brains scan our immediate horizon and when such an event comes up that matches or resonates with the negative event which we have recorded, then it kicks in as an emotional impulse and it is through that impulse that we "see" what we think is going on rather than the actual event. It is like a filter that we look through -like sunglasses and we are convinced that what we see through these sunglasses is the whole truth and nothing but the truth. It is that so and so person that is making me mad/angry. Meanwhile, it is not that particular thing that is the problem but rather us looking through the sunglasses and seeing what we think is indeed this past event that is kicking in (through the same resonance) the mechanism. It is this past negative event that is, what it is that we are "seeing" and not the person/event/situation in front of us. Accepting this, it then follows that every time we have a reaction to an event it has absolutely nothing to do with that person/event/situation in-front of us, it has everything to do with us (our past unresolved issues).

The mirror of the Universe is so honest and accurate that your deepest secrets show up in the reflections you see of yourself. Everything and every situation in your life is a mirror of an aspect of yourself, good or bad, positive or negative. The Law of Reflection reminds us to look in the mirror and change ourselves. It could be that you have unshed tears or unresolved emotional issues.

The law of reflection as explained by science - Light is known to behave in a very predictable manner. That is, the angle of incidence equals the angle of reflection. We understand that when a ray of light strikes a plane mirror, the light ray reflects off the mirror. Reflection involves a change in direction of the light ray. The convention used to express the direction of a light ray is to indicate the angle which the light ray makes with a normal line drawn to the surface of the mirror. The angle of incidence is the angle between this normal line and the incident ray; the angle of reflection is the angle between this normal line and the reflected ray.

Understanding the law of reflection can help you create a happy and joyous life. Whatever comes into your life, look into the mirror and see what it has to teach you. Once you understand the Law of Reflection you will effortlessly create wealth and prosperity in your life because it will reveal your true value.

Scientists researching body image have done eye-tracking studies, in which people are asked to stare in the mirror. Subjects don't look at anything they think is good; they just stare at their so-called faults.

Nancy Etcoff, PhD, author of *Survival of the Prettiest: The Science of Beauty,* and a Harvard Medical School psychologist had the following responses to an article on appearance and happiness:

"It would really be a good idea when you have a nice belly. I really wish that I can do this because my low self esteem comes from the man I'm married to. He looks at naked women on the Internet"

"I for one hate looking in the mirror because I'm short and out of shape, I don't feel very good about myself. And women don't find me appealing because of my size".

"Most of my 20's and 30's were spent being embarrassed about my looks because I didn't look like everyone else. I was constantly trying to brainstorm ways to get enough money to have a nose job or change my face shape".
"I have low self-esteem issues because I lived all my life in a poor neighbourhood. I need someone to help me figure out why I'm so down on myself all the time"

"I have suffered from low self esteem all of my life and I am going to be 40 years old this year".

"I have the hardest time getting motivated to take care of myself. I do not like what I see in my mirror. I don't even try clothes on in the stores anymore. I take them home and try them on and if they don't fit, I just take them back or not".

"How do you even begin the process of loving what you see because I know that this has a bigger impact on my life and those around me"

Does any of the above sound familiar to you?

According to Oprah, her emotional turmoil led to her weight problem. She said the reason she gained so much weight in the first place and the reason she had such a sorry history of abusive relationships with men was because she needed approval so much. She said she needed everyone to like her because she didn't like herself much. So she ended up with cruel self-absorbed men who told her how selfish she was. She felt they were right and was grateful to them. She said she had no sense that she deserved anything else. (George Mair, Oprah Winfrey: The Real Story)

This is how the law of reflection manifest itself. It is a message for you to look at what is going on, on the inside, and resolve it. Something like "would you please see me now? Look at me for what I am and resolve me".   What most people do is to ignore this message and assume that it is that person / event / situation in front of them that is the source of their irritation/anger. By not addressing this issue internally, you perpetuate the situation and it has a negative impact on your life such as, always being angry or fearful for example, or flaring up over nothing, or not engaging with things or holding back and afraid to have a big vision, etc.

These messages you received in the mirror are gifts that you should accept. When you don't address these messages, they sit there and wait for the next opportunity for you to be presented with. They can also become part of your system and so you will constantly attract various situations, giving you yet again an opportunity to look at your personal issues and resolve them. If over a very long period of time you don't resolve these issues, then you become sick from them. You could develop a diseases like cancer, diabetes, depression etc. This is nature's way to eventually force us to address our issues. This is not to say people that are suffering from these diseases have issues but most of the time, that is the case. When you resolve past events within yourself, you dissolve the events in your bodies and then you find that all future similar events don't provoke a response from within you and therefore you are able to address the situation without the emotional loading. What will also happen is that you don't attract that kind of situation to yourself anymore. That means you are less likely to get angry, fearful, guilty, protective, feel that you must always do things for others, be responsible for others, etc, anymore in those kinds of situations. You are then able to cope with life's situations much easier and you find that you can handle things like stress, confrontation or fearful situations as well as be assertive, manage responsibility, manage your own power, take on and manage positions of authority and so forth. When you can do this, then you open yourself up to all sorts of opportunities which will lead to your life being more productive, happier, become more comfortable with life, make more friends etc, etc. The list is endless. All of the afore-mentioned is possible when you decide to address that which is inside of you, that which you placed there, and that which is holding you back. There is no better investment to make than to do an internal clean up. The upside is unlimited for you. The downside is that you stay where you are, maybe even go down further. The choice is your. You need to clean up what is lurking below!! When you do that, you are free!

This is Oprah Winfrey's testimony when she read the autobiography of Maya Angelou, *I Know Why the Caged Bird Sings*. She admitted she had to read the book over and over. She had never before read a book that validated her own existence. She began to get her life back on track, concentrating on her education and public speaking. Oprah's talent started to take her places and shortly after that she won an Elk's Club speaking competition, earning a 4 year college scholarship as the prize. She learned that if you want to make something of yourself you had to fight.

"All that a man achieves and all that he fails to achieve is the direct result of his own thoughts."

James Allen

The law of reflection when not used properly make some people stagnant for a long time and in particular roles/positions. Let us say for instance, you are working in an organisation and there is an opportunity for a promotion. You have worked hard and have good records. That is when the mirror sends you those messages e.g. "I am not good enough", "I can't lead because I am short" and then you begin to develop the conviction that you will not get the job. These thought patterns gradually form a belief system in your subconscious mind that will most certainly guarantee that you will not get the promotion. Why? Because your unresolved events will conspire to hold you back!

As an entrepreneur, no matter how vibrant your idea is, it will be difficult to bring it to fruition if these thought patterns occur. In most cases it is even difficult to have a great idea because you will not trust your inner mind in the first instance. This may also account for why some small businesses fail or some big organisation gradually collapse due to change in leadership.

The summary of this is that whatever you see in the mirror is what you sell to your clients. When some people tell me they are passionate about their business or idea, I start to look out for the passion. People need to see your passion, touch it, feel it and hear it. Don't forget that when you start your business, you wear all the hats. Your employees need to feel your passion. Passion transmits positive energy: It is contagious.

The law of reflection is so vital that it cannot be explained in one chapter of a book. It is the foundation of any individual who desires to make an impact in the world. The trick is that when the messages show up, accept it and deal with it. In most cases you will need professional or spiritual help to lead you through the process until you begin to see something else in the mirror. After which you need absolute clarity on your objectives; a solid plan to get you there and then you must believe that you are destined to achieve them. As time passes, you must continuously reinforce this belief in your own mind.

"Education begins the gentleman, but reading, good company and reflection must finish him".

-John Locke

The interesting thing is that we tend to observe the world from a very narrow point of view - which is that obstacles are negative. In fact, obstacles can help us to grow and therefore can be positive! They are absolutely essential for growth. Sometimes things go awry and it isn't until much later that we discover that, whatever the setback was, it was there for a good reason. We learn and become stronger from the experience. Once you are able to learn to persevere in the face of all obstacles, eventually you will create the reality that you desire.

What You Can Do

Below are some action exercises to help you in this area:

- Get rid of any unresolved events. This requires a lot of honest internal self searching to find and eliminate. It is advisable to get professional and/or spiritual help for this process.

- Do not feel guilty. Forgive yourself for past "failures". Do not dwell on the past. Forgive others and avoid guilt, as it is one of the biggest destroyers of focus and confidence.

- Write down what you love about yourself or life. You can glue this to a wall and read them to yourself at least twice a day. E.g. 'I have a beautiful face', 'I am successful'.

- Begin by loving yourself first then share the love with others; not the other way around. You must love yourself free of conditions and not be judgmental or continually beating yourself up. Learn how to respect and honour yourself more deeply and identify where you need to communicate with yourself more openly and honestly

- Be grateful each and every day for your progress and what you have been able to achieve.

- Look for positive and inspiring quotes and begin to programme them into your system. As you begin to affirm these words, you will start to believe that you are destined to be successful in whatever areas you desire.

- Begin to help people genuinely and in so doing, you will be sending out positive energy. Lean to say 'I am sorry'.

- Be mindful of what you say. What do you say about yourself? What do you say about others? Do not engage in gossip about others or continue passing on hearsay. Do not engage in negative name calling or take things personally.

- Get into the habit of acting as though you have already accomplished your goals and are the success you want to be. Your new behaviour will influence the messages you receive in the mirror, which in turn will help you to realise your dreams faster! Remember, all of these are energetic vibrations which ultimately manifest as form in your life.

- Some therapists have also recommended things like enrolling in a dance class, exercise, drink a lot of water and immerse yourself in water (swimming or having a bath)

Like in Oprah's example, from the very moment she discovered her natural flair and passion for broadcasting, she directed all her energy towards feeding that passion. It was her passion for what she was doing that drew people in and made her so appealing to audiences worldwide. Oprah's passion conveys authenticity, it sends out positive energy which allows people to get an inside glimpse into her true self and garners a sense of trust between her and her audience.

There is no mystery to achieving success - it is available to all of us. You only need to be aware of, understand and, most importantly, live in accordance with these natural Laws! Everything works out perfectly by law. Things only look like coincidences and accidents to those who do not see the truths behind them. Remember you are provided with an infinite amount of possibilities and opportunities but they do not create your life, you do.

What is it that big idea you will consciously choose to birth? It's your choice – you are the Co-Creator of your world!

CHAPTER TWO

THE LAW OF VISION

*"The most pathetic person in
the world is someone who
has sight but no vision."
- Helen Keller*

In the heart of the infamous Rivonia in 1963, Nelson Mandela whilst conducting his own defence concluded his submission with the following statement: *"During my lifetime I have dedicated myself to the struggle of the African people. I have fought against white domination and I have fought against black domination. I have cherished the ideal of a democratic and free society in which all persons live together in harmony and with equal opportunities. It is an ideal which I hope to live for and to achieve. But if need be, it is an ideal for which I am prepared to die".*

Upon his release after spending 27 years in prison, Mandela rose to become the first black South African to hold the presidential office. He also received numerous awards from many nations and international institutions including the Nobel Peace Prize. Today, Mandela's vision has successfully created a legacy for multiracial, impartial democracy which is the form of government several societies in the contemporary world have failed to produce.

Let's face it not everyone has what it takes. We may not have someone like Nelson Mandela for another decade or more. What I found fascinating about his character is that he had a vision he was prepared to die for! This is the vision I am referring to in this book. I know you are familiar with the word vision and the word 'vision board' is mostly mentioned in most, if not all, of the sales training or goal setting classes. It is about shaping the future and being significant and when you do, success will automatically follow you.

Vision institutes the framework and the structure for the future you are attempting to create.

In times past, the human life revolved around seeking for the basics of life – food, clothing and shelter. Every one of us engage in one form of activity or another with the aim to create material and emotional security for ourselves, our families, and our communities. As humanity's consciousness evolves, we no longer work just to eat and clothe ourselves but to live good lives, to be fulfilled, to impact our communities and the world at large. As a matter of fact, people are beginning to have strong desires to use the powers within them to create a sustainable world. These desires to change our world and live a meaningful life by being creative has clouded our judgement that we sometimes do the right things the wrong way or using wrong motives.

In essence, from an entrepreneurial point of view, before you embark on a venture, you need to decide where you want it to be in the future. Vision is about where, how and what you want to be in the future. The same way you have a personal vision, your business must also have a vision.

Let us look at the exchange between Alice and the Cheshire Cat - in the 'Alice in Wonderland' book.

"Would you tell me, please, which way I ought to go from here?"

"That depends a good deal on where you want to get to," said the Cat.
"I don't much care where–" said Alice.

"Then it doesn't matter which way you go," said the Cat.

"–so long as I get SOMEWHERE," Alice added as an explanation.

"Oh, you're sure to do that," said the Cat, "if you only walk long enough."

Vision takes you THERE not SOMEWHERE. When you know where you are going, it's easy for you to work out or ask questions about how to get there so that when you get there, you know for sure 'This is it'. Let's say for instance, you have an interview for a job or business prospect, will any road take you there? Even if you are just starting out in business, beginning with your vision will help to decide on the scope of your business. So perhaps you just want it to remain a family business. While there is room for optimisation and small incremental change, highly successful people know that in order to be significant, you need some big vision.

"Good business leaders create a vision, articulate the vision, passionately own the vision and relentlessly drive it to completion."

- Jack Welch

In the previous chapter, we looked at how the law of reflection is the principal engine that will propel an individual to take a stand in the first instance. When choosing or deciding a vision for yourself or business, you have to understand that your past is somewhat irrelevant. The key question is, "What do you want to be?" And that question may, in fact, lead to something completely different than what you've been. As you continue to look into the law of reflection, it propels you to think and act boldly. In essence, it can completely change who you were/are, and is what will enable you to prosper year after year. According to Fortune magazine, Steve Jobs, the former CEO of Apple, has essentially changed four industries; computers, music, movies and mobile phones and his bold vision meant that Apple grew from a $5billion company in 2000 to a $170 billion by 2009.

When you look at the mirror of the universe (the law of reflection), the person you see will be determined by the vision you have, your boldness and the risk you are prepared to take. It is as simple as that. It is a natural law that is not a respecter of persons. As you grow in life and increase in knowledge, look into the mirror again and you will realise it is time to take another bold step. Your vision is not static, it can be refined as you grow in life.

What You Can Do

Below are some action exercises, which you can put in place immediately, to help you in this area:

- **Be focused**. Highly successful people are focused. A focused entrepreneur clearly knows what problems he/she is solving; has well defined markets and a very good description of their customers. When you are clear about this, then you are able to articulate why you exist in very simple terms. Being focused will help you to identify how best to grow yourself and your business.

- **Fragment your vision**. While it might be impossible to predict the future, it is advisable to have a short, medium and long term goals. Ensure that all are in alignment and that all parts are heading in the same direction and are mutually supporting and not undermining your bigger picture.

- **Learn to say NO!** Some entrepreneurs claim they are opportunity focused but you wonder whether they evaluate which opportunities they should pursue. While opportunities are good for business, it can also be a death trap for your vision if not properly evaluated. In the case of Mandela, he was offered a conditional release from prison by the government but he turned down the offer and opted to stay in his cold, dark prison cell. Half a decade later, he was released unconditionally and rose to become the president of the country. So, always carefully assess the opportunities you are offered.

- **Enrol in the school of risk.** If you want to be significant and at the same time be successful, set bigger targets. You don't necessarily have to take a course on risk but you can begin by learning from people or companies that are making significant impact and ask yourself "how did they do it?" Learn to train your mind to take bold moves you see other people take and if they can do it, why can't you?

I discovered that highly successful people have very simple visions around a major potential or a single objective. That vision often capitalises on their most important passion or trait. Mandela in his autobiography, *The Long Walk to Freedom,* traced his stubbornness to his father who was removed as the Chief of Mvevo when he refused to obey a local magistrate's insolent biddings. Clear visions usually have a clear definition, who they are influencing and often states what problem they are solving. It is clear that Mandela definitely has a distaste for injustice. What do you have distaste for? Are you prepared, like Mandela, to die for it? If you have answers to these questions then I urge you to be focused and develop a clear vision for them and success will be guaranteed.

CHAPTER THREE

THE LAW OF VALUE

*"Try not to become a man
of success. Rather
become a man of value."*

- Albert Einstein

The first step to creating value is to know what it is. And few people know what it really is, most times they misconstrue it to be money. What is value? How do you create it? If I were to put it in simple terms, being in a job or having a business is not about money as most people think, it's about exchange of values. Let us start with money: It is merely legal tender, a physical representation that we use to exchange the value within us. For without the value within, what can the value of a thing, such as a house, be to us? The material things have no "money" value in themselves—we give that to them. That means for you to have or continue to have money, there has to be continuous flow and exchange of value within you and other people.

So if you desire to be very rich or successful, all you need to do is develop your internal value, give this value to others to help them create value in themselves and in return your physical representation of value 'money' will increase continuously. In essence, when you offer a product or service for sale, it has a value to the customer. As an employee, your skills add value to your employers value. The question is, how do you turn the value within you to a product or service that people will buy in order to create value for themselves? I suggest the first key questions are to find out what problems you are solving and how important it is to the customers?

Let us take for instance Anita Roddick, an entrepreneur and founder of The Body Shop, a cosmetics company that shaped ethical consumerism in the UK and around the world. Anita was known for her campaign against the role the media and the beauty industry play to make women unhappy about how they look like and how the female body is portrayed to be in need of repair. Anita's value was centred around the fact that:

- there is no cream in the world that will restore youth to a 50 – year – old woman
- stretch marks and wrinkles show how women have worked hard, raised kids and struggled- they are necessary symptoms of what add value to women's lives

With the above in mind, she redefined the perception of beauty, legitimised the ageing process and spread a new message. For The Body Shop, beauty is a healthy part of everyday life. It is an active, outward expression of everything a woman like about herself. The company celebrates women rather than idealise them. The cosmetics promote health rather than glamour, reality rather than the dubious promise of instant rejuvenation. In offering her value as a product, the company makes innovative beauty products without testing them on animals, without destroying the planet, and without exploiting the people that made them. Anita opened the first Body Shop in 1976, by 2004 it had 1980 stores, serving over 77 million customers throughout the world. In 2006, the business was purchased by L'Oreal for £652 million. The Body Shop was voted the second most trusted brand in the United Kingdom, and 28th top brand in the world.

"We make a living by what we get, we make a life by what we give."

- Sir Winston Churchill

Here is an example of how we can translate the value within us into a product that add value to others and in exchange for your physical value – money. Creating or adding value in simple term means giving. From the bestselling book, 'The Go-Giver', the authors (Bob Burg and John David Mann) described 'giving' as the secret to success. We often hear of someone being described as a "go-getter." It brings up the thought of a successful and determined person who will stop at nothing to get to the top. The book – 'The Go-Giver' is a parable about a young man called Joe, a true "go-getter", who is ambitious and desperately wants to be successful. The problem is that the harder he works, the further away he is from his goal of being successful. Joe comes to the end of a bad sales quarter and becomes desperate to land a key sale, so he seeks leverage and clout from a legendary consultant, called Pindar. What Joe gets instead, from Pindar and his friends, is lessons on "go-giving". Pindar tells Joe "Most people just laugh when they hear that the secret to success is giving…Then again, most people are nowhere near as successful as they wish they were." Pindar and his friends share with Joe, the Five Laws of Stratospheric Success, and Joe learns that changing his focus from getting to giving leads to unexpected returns.

In the book, Pindar tells Joe "All the great fortunes in the world have been created by men and women who had a greater passion for what they were giving – their product, service or idea – than what they were getting. Their definition of the law of value is that; your true worth is determined by how much more you give in value than you take in payment". This explains that we are not giving more than we receive in payment, but we are adding more value to people that we serve. It comes from a deep desire to really make a difference in the lives of those around us and we cannot view it as a formula for success but instead a way of life.

Although there are so many books and articles on success, creating substantial value can be very overwhelming! The problem is that a lot of these books focus on getting rather than giving so you must ensure that you find principles that align with your values and empower you to develop a successful business with a mindset of serving and giving.

Let us look at the example below:

"The company I started did research and market entry consulting for companies wanting to enter Asian markets, particularly Japan. After more than six years of ferociously hard work, we received a multi-million-dollar buyout offer. This was all new to me because when I started, I didn't even know people sold companies. Anyway, I paid off three mortgages, maxed out the kids' college funds, took the family on a great vacation, and invested the remainder to provide passive income. But like everyone else, I still faced the big question: 'What am I going to do with the rest of my life?' In a way, that question grew tougher precisely because I'd been relieved of the pressing need to earn a living. Seeking answers sharpened my awareness that work is about more than achieving financial independence.

I think most successful entrepreneurs feel the same way. I've talked with a lot of people who, collectively, have sold dozens of companies for amounts ranging from one to $40 million U.S. Not a single one ever mentioned "achieving financial independence" as their primary motivation for working.

Fortune-seekers can rarely sustain their passion through the hard times. Successful enterprises are

laser-focused on Value Provided to Customers. Entrepreneurship is not about you; it's about effectively serving others" - Carl James, Entrepreneur
Source: Business Model You Preview

I agree with Carl that achieving financial independence is not a primary motivation for working. There is so much inside you to give. You have more value capability within you than you could possibly experience in a lifetime. You can never reach your limit of creating or adding value and you do not need to worry about how to convert your internal value into your external value 'money'; as you will see, it will happen automatically. All you need to do is to be a person of value, that is be 'giving focused'. Some people give time, they volunteer to support different causes and in so doing they become successful and ultimately significant. In the previous chapter, we saw that Mandela didn't create any product or service, he propelled his vision by simply giving himself, he spent over two decades in prison and you know the rest of the story.

When you have a mindset of giving, exercise it daily, act on it, become it and situations and opportunities will automatically present themselves for the equivalent conversion into money. None of the highly successful people today could have in their early years possibly predicted and planned the exact sequence of events that would lead to their immense wealth. They probably had a vision, a set of goals and a plan, but very few of them will tell you that they met countless opportunities that "joined the dots" for them in ways they could never have predicted. Their goals were their own doing but the paths that led to their massive wealth was as a result of their constantly looking for ways to give.

"Tricks & Treachery are the practice of fools that have not wit enough to be honest."

- Ben Franklin

Rather than thinking about what you can sell to make money, change your thoughts to how you can add value to other people's lives. I believe that the overarching purpose of our lives is helping others. Even though your purpose is to make money, you can only achieve this by creating services or products that help people in some way. We discussed previously that personal or business vision is essential on your part to becoming a person of significance. It is this vision that guides the design of your value into a product or service. In that sense, having a vision is crucial. After all, no business or individual can exist to be all things to all people. And the sooner you identify your value, the faster you will grow.

So, how can you go about creating the kind of value that can translate to physical value? There are three action exercises, which you can put in place immediately, to help you in this area:

- The first step is to **Assess** your current situation. You can begin by asking yourself questions like "Am I enjoying my business"? "Am I interested in my work?". Often times when coaching entrepreneurs, I discover that there exist a mismatch between the clients (who they are) and their business (what they do). If you find yourself in this kind of mismatch, I suggest you look into the law of reflection to identify who you truly are. Follow the guide listed and seek help if you feel you can't do it on your own. I always recommend that people seek help from professionals at the initial stage and then they can progress on their own. An individual on a path to being significant should be able to articulate Who they are, How they help, and Who they help.

- The next stage is to **Align** your internal value with your daily activities. If your value or an important skill or set of abilities are missing in your daily activities, there is a tendency to lose money (physical value)and this might also result in dissatisfaction with life or your organisation, some sort of illness e.g. stress or depression. For instance in stage 1 above, you assessed yourself and identified what your internal value (s) is, the next thing to do is to look for how you add that value, ability or skill to your daily activities.

To some people, it could be their voice, I guess such a person will look for ways to use that voice either through singing, broadcasting, motivational speaking. Most of the named celebrities in the music industry actually started their singing career from their local church. By using it often, you then become master of it and makes it easier to turn the internal value into physical value – money. In case you are dissatisfied with your current situation, identify why you are dissatisfied – you will find that this is as a result of an internal value that is crying to be expressed. You need to examine the reasons why you are not utilising that value – perhaps you might need to revisit the law of reflection. Look at what the mirror is telling you.

- The last exercise is to **Acquire**. In the last chapter we discussed having a big vision. While there is no harm in having a big vision, if there is a mismatch of value, this will also lead to dissatisfaction, illness etc. The point here is, when you have a huge vision, there is every possibility that you do not possess all the internal value required for the translation of the vision into physical value. What you do in a situation like that is to acquire partners or employees, who have the personalities and internal value that are compatible with your vision. when you attend a job interview and you are asked the question 'why do you want to work for this organisation' or 'why are you applying for this role?' the key point is to check if your internal value harmonises with the activities that will be required to deliver the physical value.

Remember that you have a unique internal value within and you can create products or services that are unique to you by using this value. The exchange of these unique creations is what brings about the physical value - money. Hence money is just a medium of exchange for our uniquely developed internal value. Engaging in cheating, squeezing, manipulating and taking advantage of people, paying employees less than what they deserve, coveting other people's property, envy, and the like can create temporary external value - money, but you cannot rise to your full potential this way, and indeed, you may even fall. If you want to build external wealth, build internal value and then exercise it. It is that simple.

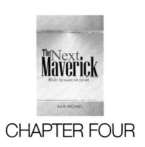

CHAPTER FOUR

THE LAW OF DIFFERENCE

"To be yourself in a world that is constantly trying to make you something else is the greatest accomplishment."

-Ralph Waldo Emerson

Conventionality can be your worst enemy. If you do what everybody does, you will get what everybody gets. Every day, people get up in the morning; they go to work and do things like everybody else and can't really explain the reason why they do what they do. I once met a lady who works so hard, doing like three different jobs and her reason was that everybody works hard. Her other reason was that she had to pay her bills, provide for herself and her family. Research revealed that about 1.4billion people live in poverty. When we hear of poverty, we think of the under developed or developing countries. According to Food and Agriculture Organisation (FAO, 2012) developed regions also saw the number of hungry people rise from 13 million in 2004-2006 to 16 million in 2010-2012.

Have you ever wondered why the vast majority of people today are not successful or financially independent? I believe they could be if only they did not do things like everyone else did. In order to get something better you have to do things differently, after all that is the essence of being significance. When you survey average people against highly successful people, you can almost always realise a connection between those that are "just like everyone else," versus those who are "uniquely different." The temptation for many entrepreneurs is that they keep trying to do what everyone else is doing, "just a little bit better." Unfortunately, looking like everyone else isn't a recipe for success. Being different (in a way that your target market appreciates) is a much better path to success.

History has recorded a number of people who dared to be different in their chosen field. In their time on earth they pursued, with intense focus, their vision and changed the world and pushed the human race forward. From Albert Einstein, Bob Dylan, Martin Luther King Jr., Buckminster Fuller, Thomas Edison, Ted Turner, Maria Callas, Mahatma Ghandi, Amelia Earhart, Alfred Hitchcock, Martha Graham, Pablo Picasso, Frank Lloyd Wright, the list is endless. Can you tell what they have in common? They are not fond of rules and they have no respect for the status quo. You can call them the round pegs in the square holes, the troublemakers, disagree with them or glorify them. About the only thing you can't do is ignore them because they change things. They are the ones who see things differently. You might call them the crazy ones, yes they were crazy enough to think they could change the world and they did. They push the human race forward.

One person I am going to add to the list above is no other than the geek who founded Apple and became one of the richest and most powerful men in the world. Steve Jobs was given up for adoption at birth, he dropped out of college after one semester and at the age of twenty-one he created Apple in his parents' garage with his friend Steve Wozniack. Through Pixar, the iPod and the iPhone, Jobs revolutionised the major industries of movies, music, and phones. He became Apple's guru and godfather for groundbreaking innovations, changed many industries and changed consumers' attitudes about technology by making computers more accessible and friendly for the masses. He was able to craft himself with the iconic "Think Different."

"Be yourself, everyone else is taken"
- Oscar Wilde

The ability to be different from others is dependent on the internal value that you possess; we have already established this in the previous chapter. The fact that you have this value in you does not necessarily mean that someone else is not permitted to possess it. What makes the 'difference' is the ability to turn that internal value into a product or service to clients (for them to derive value) and ultimately in exchange for the physical value – money.

Like most entrepreneurs, Steve Jobs compete in mature market - the world of computer. He was not the inventor but he managed to carve out a place in the market and grow rapidly. That tells you that you don't have to be an inventor to be different; as a matter of fact everything that we need is already created. We will discuss more on this in the law of creativity.

The market place is crowded with 'me-too' products and services. The same could be said for the work place and this is part of the reason why some organisations have high turnover of employees and possibly responsible for high rate of unemployment. With little to differentiate them, employers will simply treat them as a commodity and employ the one who is the most convenient or the cheapest. For entrepreneurs, your way out of this 'me–too' trap is to identify a niche market and develop products and services which better match the needs of the target market. This is not about competition with others. It is about having the foresight to know that customers want something and seizing the opportunity to create it for them. We often hear about collaborations, joint ventures etc. because people have realised we are all different and unique in some ways and so perhaps there is the need for more than the bog standard. In a bid to be different, some organisations have created their value in terms of product/service quality, friendliness, level of helpfulness and all alter their customers feeling during and after an experience.

If you ask me, once you have mastered the first three laws, without effort, you will be able to identify how different you are from others and use this knowledge to create products and services that meet the needs of the people you are sent to.

"Your time is limited, so don't waste it living someone else's life."
- Steve Jobs

I have put together three exercises you can do to help differentiate you from the crowd.

- **Be honest**. "To thine own self be true" is Polonius's last piece of advice to his son Laertes (Shakespeare, Hamlet). What does it mean to be "true"? it simply means be "loyal to your own best interests. Take care of yourself first, and that way you'll be in a position to take care of others. The problem with most people is that they try to be all things to all people. This is suicidal and hardly will you see anyone making an impact using such methods. The first step is to do an honest analysis of yourself, if you follow the instructions listed in the first three chapters, it will be easier for you to find out your unique features, skills, abilities etc. Once you have done an honest analysis and identify your unique value, develop expertise in this area. Be known to be a problem solver of a particular problem. Let us take the human body for example, we have professionals who specialise in the treatment of the eyes, teeth, brain etc. Many businesses have taken advantage of this and grown substantial market presence by solving an especially difficult problem which requires specific expertise.

- **Be realistic.** Once you have identified your unique value, you have to accept the fact that it will not appeal to everyone. No matter how great a product is, that does not mean it will be universally acceptable or adopted. What you then need to do is to look for people who appreciate this value. Until you put your value to use, you will not appreciate your difference. This is what is referred to as creating a niche market. If the South Africans were not groaning for freedom, Mandela's imprisonment would have been a futile effort. Here is what House Majority Leader Eric Cantor of the United States of America had to say in his tribute to Steve Jobs: "There is not a day that goes by, and often not an hour, that a Steve Jobs invention does not better my family's life." Don't be discouraged when people don't buy into your idea, some people are quick to change businesses or profession just because of a few rejections. The fact that it does not appeal to them doesn't mean it won't appeal to someone else. That doesn't mean it is not needed. Someone needs you that is why you are in this world.

- **Be consistent**. Whatever you say you will do, do it. Whoever you say you are, be it. This is the language of being different. Give a clear, concise and consistent message. That way, every time people hear from you they receive a consistent message that, over time, will burn its way into their memories. Successful entrepreneurs only maintain their position by carrying out continual customer analysis to ensure the organisation's products and services continue to deliver what it promises to deliver. You will need to be able to offer reasonable proof of that assertion.

Whatever your product, service or cause is, study the subject and be sure. It is hard to create something when you're not sure what it looks like. Internal value is different from knowledge. Knowledge will validate your value, it will make it meaningful and sufficiently important to your target audience.

While being different is important to success (think Apple), the key is to be different in a way that appeals to your target audience. In other words, there is no point being different when you do not have followers. That means you are sent to meet the particular needs of some people in some regions at a particular time. The essence of being different will be revealed in the next chapter.

CHAPTER FIVE

THE LAW OF INFLUENCE

The greatest ability in business is to get along with others and to influence their actions.

-John Hancock

Many people think of Thomas Edison when it comes to the person who invented the light bulb. The light bulb wasn't his idea, but he was able to make one that was good enough to influence the world. He is accredited with making many other inventions that have also greatly influenced the world and have the most influence on the way we live our lives today. When the light bulb was invented, the lives of people back then were transformed. These people were used to lights from candles, oil lamps and fireplaces. Today we are used to the light bulb and can be bought in shops everywhere, the light bulb can be found in many of our devices. Now we can leave the light bulb on while we are out without the fear of burning down the house.

By now you understand that in order to be 'different' you need to research and learn more about your value. The knowledge you gain through research will help you to be able to create a unique product or service. Edison spent his childhood learning new things and working on them. Even though he went to formal school for only three months and was taught at home by his mother, he was still able to learn a lot of things just by reading. Through his knowledge and a different way of thinking, he was able to invent many useful devices. I mentioned in the previous chapters that we are in this world on an assignment. Our internal value will only be converted to external value-money, when we give that value to people that need it. No one asked Thomas

Edison to make any of his inventions after all, people were accustomed to the candle lights etc., before he invented the light bulb. According to him, he tried 10,000 times but never recorded them as failed attempts. Because of his persistent questioning and his thirst for knowledge, he was able to become one of the greatest inventors in the world.

Highly successful people have a very clear definition of who they are, what they do and where they are going. They are going THERE not SOMEWHERE. They know exactly what problems they are solving and they know how and where to deliver solutions to the people in a way which will create a positive experience for them. Above all else, they go out and touch lives, they don't wait to be found, they position themselves by aligning their daily activities with their vision. They provide a solution to the problem which the people or target audience have. While there were other countries that were fighting for justice, Mandela did not represent all of them even though his victory and legacies were examples worth emulating by leaders globally. He understood the pain of his people, he was one of them and so his destination and desire was clear. You need to identify specific people / audience / customers / organisations who have a problem which you can solve. They are either locally or regionally based, identified by gender, race or other groups. You cannot effectively have influence unless your internal value has an effect (positive) on certain group of people.

The challenge now is, you have this great idea which you have either turned into a product or service but you don't know how you can influence your audience. How do you get people to support your idea? How many minutes, hours, days or months does it take you to make up your mind about a decision? If you find it a herculean task to influence yourself, how do you then influence others? Let us face it influencing others can be challenging, which is why it is worth understanding the psychological principles behind the influencing process.

Have you noticed how after watching a TV advert from an attractive person of the opposite sex, that you have no recollection whatsoever what was advertised nor be able to grab a line? There is some obvious psychology behind this simple experience, and it is just one example to show us how human beings are so easily and predictably influenced either for good or bad.

To explain this process we will be using the Six Principles of Influence. The Six Principles of Influence (also known as the Six Weapons of Influence) were created by Robert Cialdini, Regents Professor Emeritus of Psychology and Marketing at Arizona State University. He published them in his respected 1984 book "Influence: The Psychology of Persuasion."

The principles are: Reciprocity, Commitment, Social proof, Liking, Authority and Scarcity. It must be said though that these are not the only tool you can use to influence people. You can always use them in conjunction with other tools but understanding these principles will help you to quickly identify when people try to manipulate you. Also be careful not to use them to mislead or deceive people and sell unethical products.

Before you can effectively use these principles to influence others, it is important that you understand your audience and that you know why you want to influence them. Think about your ultimate objectives, and decide which principles will be most useful in your circumstances.

We'll now explore the six principles:

1. **Reciprocity**: Reciprocity is referred to as a mutual interchange of favours or privileges. When we discussed the law of value, we mentioned that you have to give first in order to receive. In essence you have to be seen as a 'go-giver' rather than a 'go-getter.' By nature, we are wired to return favours, treat others as they treat us etc. Based on the concept of reciprocity, this can lead some people to feel obliged to offer compensation or return favours to others if they have received such gestures from them. This is because we are uncomfortable with feeling indebted to them.

   So how can you apply reciprocity to influence others; firstly think of your objective or purpose? Ensure you have a good motive, then you will need to identify a specific problem which has a compelling need to be solved. You then need to identify what you can give to them in return. Depending on the relevance and how great your product or service is (value), people will be willing to pay a reasonable price (external value) to satisfy their need. Remember that you can also use this principle by simply providing specific information which can demonstrate how the product or service can readily solve your audience's problems.

2. **Commitment (and Consistency):** Cialdini says that we have a deep desire to be consistent. For this reason, when we have committed to something, we are then more likely to go through with it. I am sure you are familiar with stakeholder engagement; the idea is to get people's commitment early on, either verbally or in writing. Let us say for example, you are building support for a project that involves people suffering from a particular disease. The best way to go about it is to engage with people (sufferers or those having an interest) early on, get their views or feedback and get their commitments. The same applies to products or services. Many companies can trace some of their sales to their free product offers or complimentary consultations given to customers. It is also an avenue to get feedback on how to improve their product or service. Among many of his inventions during his life was an electric vote recording machine which turned out to be a disaster. Of course, Edison later improved on his work which led him to invent the quadruplex transmitter. He was committed.

3. **Social Proof**: This principle relies on people's sense of "safety in numbers." For example, people are more likely to eat in a restaurant if it is busy. The assumption is that if lots of people are doing it, then it must be good. Just as people will advertise on a site which has more hits, you are likely to purchase a product when you speak to people who are familiar with it or similar to you. The beauty industries have succeeded in using this method. You can use this principle by creating a "buzz" around your idea or product. The easiest way to do it now is by using social media. Many businesses and professionals have raised their profiles using this platform. Highlight the number of people using your products or service, get plenty of testimonials, encourage people to talk about it using social media, and publish case studies with current customers to demonstrate its success.

4. **Liking**: Cialdini says that we are more likely to be influenced by people we like. This is not surprising as people are drawn to personal branding. Customers want to buy from you when they know you and what you can do. They want to relate with your story, they want to see if there is a connection, they want to know if they can trust you. In my days working as an Accounts Manager of a 5 star hotel, this is one of the principles I adopted and it resulted in increased sales and customer loyalty.

Many international development organisations also use change agents from within the community in order to make great impact in developing regions as people are more likely to listen to people who they know and respect. However, this does not happen automatically. It takes a great deal of time and effort to be able to trust and build a rapport with clients and you will also need to be consistent with this behaviour. The key to success in this principle is to develop active listening skills; it is advisable you don't try to be liked by others for the sake of it. Remember, building relationships takes time and it normally happens in phases.

5. **Authority:** We feel a sense of duty or obligation to people in positions of authority. This is why advertisers of pharmaceutical products employ doctors to front their campaigns and why most religious people are more likely to do what their leaders tell them. Job titles, uniforms, and even accessories like cars or gadgets can lend an air of authority and can persuade us to accept what these people say. In this principle, you can use both your own authority, and the authority of others, as influencers. You need to have a proper understanding on how to use authority to influence people so that you do not use it negatively. To use authority, get support from influential and powerful people and ask for their help to support your idea. You will need to be careful so that you do not choose people simply because they are in authority because they might

not be the people's choice.

Sometimes a new business can use an existing channel to gain access to a target audience. This is often the case with joint ventures, where two or more businesses agree to work together to promote each other's products to the ultimate benefit of a joint customer.

Smart and well tailored clothing, impressive offices, well produced business stationeries can also lend authority. If you are providing a service, it is important to be seen as an authority in your area of expertise. Get knowledge, talk about impressive research or statistics, you need to be seen as a 'go-to' person.

6. **Scarcity:** This principle says that things are more attractive when their availability is limited, or when we stand to lose the opportunity to acquire them on favourable terms. Do you know that people are more likely to buy a product if they are told that it is the last one, or that a special offer will soon expire? With this principle, people need to know that they are missing out if they don't act quickly. If you're selling a product, you can limit the availability of stock, set a closing date for the offer, or create special editions of products. You can also use urgency to get support for your Project. For example, you can highlight the possible urgent consequences of the problem that your idea helps to solve or the consequence if no action is taken. Have

you ever watched a campaign on TV and you are being told how many more people will die if you don't take action? That urgency can cause you to take action.

In order to effectively influence people, your target audience must have the willingness and the ability to afford the product or service. If you are championing a cause, your research and report must be presented in ways that are compelling to get them to buy into your idea. Although you may not be limited to a geography or segment, for wide influence or global coverage to be achieved, you will need to learn to grow gradually over a number of years in your selected area.

When you have a product or service that solves a compelling need, it will be easily accepted in other geographical areas without you necessarily having to set up offices in those locations. With social media and advancement in technology; people are able to increase their wider audience globally and influence them quicker. While you might not be an inventor like Thomas Edison, you sure do have internal value and your audience are waiting to be influenced.

CHAPTER SIX

THE LAW OF TIME

"I am aware that success is more than a good idea. It is timing too".

-Anita Roddick

There are certain things we have the power to influence. As humans, we have the freewill to make a choice; whether to turn right or left, up or down, northwards or southwards. But there are some things we do not have the opportunity to choose and one of them is how we ended up here on earth. I believe that each and every one of us is here for a purpose. You are here on an assignment: You are here to influence other people. The circumstances and location you were born in are perfect for you to collect the necessary "tools" to fulfil your chosen purpose were you to go through life with such awareness. That is why your unique value, difference and vision feels so good once you discover it. That is why it gives you so much joy doing it. That is because you were chosen for it a long time ago; before you were born. It is what you came here to do.

When you are awakening to this realisation that you are here on an assignment, nothing will seem as a coincidence to you. You will view every event in your life as a pointer that leads you to the fulfilment of your purpose. You will learn to appreciate every one that you come in contact with because some are to help you on your journey. Some people, even though they were cruel to you at some point, you should see them as lessons of life which you must pass through. You will ultimately value your time and seize every moment if you are aware of this. The law of time will help you to have an understanding of time and how to use it to your advantage.

Have you heard it said, or even said it yourself: "Thirty is the new twenty"? It seems as if time has been shortened, things that were done earlier in life in the past — finishing school, landing your first "real" job, having kids, buying a house – are getting pushed back later in life. In fact, "thirty is the new twenty" is one of the biggest lies of our age. People are now awakening to their purpose. Man has begun to realise he does not exist to fulfil his basic needs. There is more to life. Man has realised his life is in his own hands. Being the architect of his fortune or misfortune (cause and effect), he might as well seize the opportunity to do the right things. Create his world – the world he would like to see. Thomas Edison believed that he didn't do any of his inventions by accident, no wonder he dropped out of school to pursue his purpose.

At age 20, Bill Gates dropped out of Harvard and co-founded Microsoft and at the same age, Sir Isaac Newton began developing a new branch of mathematics. At age 21, Thomas Alva Edison created his first invention, an electric vote recorder and at the same age, Steve Jobs co-founded Apple Inc. At age 22, Inventor Samuel Colt patented the Colt six-shooter revolver and at the same age, Cyrus Hall McCormick invented the McCormick reaper, which allowed one man to do the work of five.

At age 26, Albert Einstein published five major research papers in a German physics journal, fundamentally changing man's view of the universe and leading to such inventions as the television and the atomic bomb and at the same age, Benjamin Franklin published the first edition of *Poor Richard's Almanac*, Eli Whitney invented the cotton gin, and Napoleon Bonaparte conquered Italy. You can call it the 'hall of fame of accomplishment' but I refer to them as people who have the understanding of how time is relevant to their purpose.

In the Outliers: *The Story of Success*, a non-fiction book written by Malcolm Gladwell, he examines the factors which contribute to high levels of success. In the book, he interviews Gates, who says that unique access to a computer at a time when they were not commonplace helped him succeed. Without that access, Gladwell states that Gates would still be "a highly intelligent, driven, charming person and a successful professional", but that he might not be worth US$50 billion. While there are so many illustrations in Gladwell's book, including the 10,000-Hour Rule, what I find fascinating is the fact that when we were born, where we come from, where we are and who we have contact with all have a great influence on our level of success.

According to him, historians comb through every year in human history, looking in every corner of the world for evidence of extraordinary wealth and almost 20 percent of the names they end up with come from a single generation in a single country.

Let us look at the list of these Americans and their birth years:

John D. Rockefeller	1839
Andrew Carnegie	1835
Frederick Wayerhaeuser	1834
Jay Gould	1836
Marshall Field	1834
George F. Baker	1840
Hetty Green	1834
James G. Fair	1831
Henry H. Rogers	1840
J.P. Morgan	1837
Oliver H. Payne	1839
George Pullman	1831
Peter Arrell Brown Widener	1834
Philip Danforth Armour	1832

Source: Outliers

The names above are on the list of seventy five richest people in human history, which includes queens, kings and pharaohs. What can you deduce from the list? Think about that for a moment. The answer becomes obvious if you think about it.

Now here is Gladwell's analysis:

- Between the 1860s and 1870s, the American economy went through the greatest transformation in history
- The emergence of the Wall Street and the construction of the railroads
- The era which the rules that govern traditional economy were broken

The interpretation of this list is that your age is important during this transformation era. Hence, if you were born earlier or later; you will either be too young or too old. You would have missed it. You would not have the mind-set to see the potential that the future held.

Still don't get it? This paragraph from *Britannica* takes us back to the history of personal computers.

"Before 1970, computers were big machines requiring thousands of separate transistors. They were operated by specialized technicians, who often dressed in white lab coats and were commonly referred to as computer priesthood. The machines were expensive and difficult to use. Few people came in direct contact with them, not even their programmers. The typical interaction was as follows: a programmer coded instructions and data on preformatted paper, a keypunch operator transferred the data onto punch cards, a computer operator fed the cards into a card reader, and the computer executed the instructions or stored"

"If you keep waiting for the right time, it may never happen. Sometimes you have to make the most of the time you have."

- Priya Ardis, Ever My Merlin

I almost can't believe the process described above ever existed. Isn't it amazing that today a four year old child can operate a computer effortlessly? What went wrong? Another invention or what? Perhaps some people decided to change their world at a particular time. Let us see if the law of time is at work here.

Consider the list below of some of the influential people of our time:

Bill Gates	1955
Paul Allen	1953
Steve Ballmer	1956
Steve jobs	1955
Eric Schmidt	1955
Bill Joy	1954
Scott McNealy	1954
Vinod Khosla	1955
Andy Bechtolsheim	1955

Do you see the picture now?

History recorded that by 1976, several firms were competing to introduce the first truly successful commercial personal computers. Three machines, the Apple II, PET 2001, and TRS-80 were all released in 1977, eventually selling millions of machines. Byte magazine later referred to their launch as the "1977 Trinity".

Now let us view Gladwell's analysis:

- The important date in the history of the personal computer revolution was January 1975
- The year of the release of an extraordinary minicomputer kit to rival commercial models – Altair 8800
- That means, if you were born too early, you'll probably be established in your career, married, have kids, mortgage; Perhaps too old to seize the moment. At the same time if you were born later, you might be too young in 1975.
- Ideally to be part of the revolution, you want to be in your twenties. Using this analysis which is to say, born in 1954 or 1955.

Can you see some clear and striking patterns here? I will leave you to decide. I urge you not to be ignorant about them. Gladwell summarised it this way, "These are people given a special opportunity to work really hard and seized it, and who happened to come of age at a time when that extraordinary effort was rewarded by the rest of the society".

Highly successful people are usually created and/or supported by a major environmental change usually soon after the change has occurred or when it has reached critical mass. That is, something has happened in technology, the political environment, consumer values or in the economy which has created a gap or need. They are created or changed to satisfy an urgent or emerging need in the community usually at a time when there is an inadequate supply of solutions to meet that need. Simply put, their success occurs because there is an emerging need which cannot be satisfied by existing entrepreneurs. This gap creates a vacuum which they recognise and they provide a solution quicker than others.

While the focus is not so much about doing things at a particular age etc.; the most important thing here is that, you are the right person for your vision, irrespective of where you are in the world. It is not a coincidence that you were born into your family, the people in your life, the person sitting next to you, the organisation where you are working, etc. You are the right person. what makes the difference is the ability to seize the moment – your time is now. We have already established that you are a walking 'value' seeking opportunities to exchange that internal value with others and in return for a physical value – money. In as much as your value is needed by an audience, the time of delivery of that value is also crucial.

For example, let us assume you want to purchase an item online and you found two sellers offering home delivery both for the same amount. The difference is that one will deliver in two days while the other will take seven working days. If you are in urgent need of the product then your answer is as good as mine. Call it 'fast age' or 'jet age', people want things now! Microwave food, instant download, fast trains; every avenue that can shorten the time.

On the contrary, the human brain has been wired to think that the more time you are given, then the more important a task will seem. Also, a task that has to be finished within an hour is perceived to be of less importance. Here is what Parkinson's Law state: the law states that 'work expands to fill the time available for its completion'. Although vigorously argued by management consultants, the lesson from it is that you have the power, the choice, and the willpower to do or complete certain tasks within a time specified by you. Meaning you can actually compress time to enable you to complete a task in a given time otherwise it will take forever to complete or get it started.

This means, undertaking certain projects or tasks at the right time is critical to gaining power, seizing opportunity and ultimately driving success. This does not mean that highly successful people recognise the opportunity alone. It may be that but they are just quick to take actions and make things happen before others. They are bold to make decisions at a time which change the status quo and require people to behave differently. How many people will be bold enough to drop out of school just to pursue a dream? Well, Richard Branson, Bill Gates and other successful entrepreneurs did. While there is always an opportunity for other individuals, timely decisions usually create radical transformation that can have a major impact on the economy and dramatically affect the entire globe.

"Success is simple. Do what's right, the right way, at the right time".
-Arnold H. Glasow

So how does this apply to you? How long does it take you to make a decision? How long does it take you to complete your projects? Are you sensitive to what is happening around you? Could they be a pointer to your breakthrough? Which industry's revolution were you born to be a part of? Have you examined the people in your life, both past and present and are there any similarities?

The honest answers to these questions will help you determine your level of understanding the law of time.

The three points below will help you use the law to your advantage:

1. **Declare a state of Urgency**. If you want to know what separates highly successful people from all others, it is the speed at which they take action. Take notice of the word action. It does not mean they got it right at the first attempt but they at the end of the day, did it. Period! Like Richard Branson would say "screw it, just do it." Learn to embrace deadlines and constraints! Set the deadline yourself and hold on to it.. The world is evolving; there is less pressure on people to be perfect. Businesses can afford to make mistakes and use feedback to perfect their ideas.

   Google is a good example, they consistently generate new ideas and put them out in the world in "imperfect" form to test them and see what people think. As long as you have a working prototype out in the world, you can continue on improving your idea. Unfortunately, most people don't have this type of mindset. Being a redeemed perfectionist myself, I spent a lot of time analysing till the idea becomes paralysed. Consider the amount of time it takes from conceiving an idea to execution. Sometimes by the time you finish planning, there might not be the need for it or a smarter person has seized the time. So how about if you have an idea on Monday, you can ensure that by Wednesday plans are already in place for execution.

2. **Set standards**. While you might not have control on how people treat you, sure you can choose the way you respond. Always set a deadline when you delegate a task or outsource a task. When you examine highly successful people, you can see that they all have their roots in setting standards and overtime people will follow. What you can do is to go against the traditional rules of doing things, create your own 'terms' in order to keep things moving faster. Creating your own 'terms' and standards will help you to foresee changes in the future and also prepare you for it. That way, you are creating your own world, and can predictably capture the future.

3. **Reward Your Actions**. How many people in history have attempted to do something and failed several times. Thomas Edison finally got the bulb the 10,000th time. The fact that you are bold enough to take the risk alone is worth rewarding. Promise yourself something and let your focus be on your reward, so that it will motivate you enough to take a step. You can do the same with people; reward them for taking a step even though they may fail in the end. We will discuss more on this in the law of reward.

The important question is, "What are you going to declare as a state of urgency in your personal life or business?" Completing this book is one of mine as I have been on it for over three years! Can you imagine. It is never too late to implement that idea, can you implement it in one day? Two days? Yes you can! And when you do, you are probably going to be the next world changer. As Dr Edward Kramer says so well, "Eliminate the time between the idea and the act and your dreams will become realities."

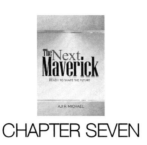

CHAPTER SEVEN

THE LAW OF CONNECTION

"Alone we can do little.
Together we can do much "
— *Helen Keller*

Highly successful people usually look at themselves honestly and see what it is that they enjoy most and what it is that they are a whole lot better at than most other people. This is an honest analysis. They are mostly the visionary even though they might not be good at marketing, selling, or anything else. They may also be good at a whole lot of other things which are not particularly relevant to their vision but can be useful in their personal life like swimming, golfing or cooking but that is beside the point. The point is that they first of all identify what it is that they are extraordinary at—not just good at, but extraordinary. The next thing is that they find out what it is that they really enjoy and cannot stop doing? All that matters is what they are better at and what they enjoy doing. Then they do only that thing and they look out for people to do everything else. They do not worry that people will not do the rest as good as they would have. Once you have a mindset that your vision is connected to other people's vision then you are on your way to becoming significant and ultimately successful. It takes greatness to give greatness: You cannot give what you don't have.

Why is it that out of every 1000 new businesses, **40%** fail within the first year, and **80%** would fail within 5 years; 80% of those businesses fail before they make it to 10 years. Even when all the external factors are extremely positive, few businesses develop to a reasonable size. That leaves us with **4%** of new businesses still around after 10 years (www.creativeoverflow.net) . If we have a growing population and demand for new products are high but market barriers are low, then you would expect there to be a great number of entrepreneurs having the capability to take advantage of the growing market.

So why do new businesses fail? You begin to wonder if there are unforeseen circumstances causing new businesses to fail as you'll also find some professionals get stuck in their career after a while. The other thing is that you find some people, after getting stuck in their career for so long, decide that it is time to venture into business. It is very popular nowadays: 'professional turn entrepreneur.' The same plumber is now an entrepreneur. Like most things in life, there is a very simple explanation for this and if you are a "Life Changer" like me, you are always looking for ways to beat the odds and not strengthen the statistics.

So, why do businesses never see their 10 year anniversary? The explanation for this is rather simple. During my research, I interviewed former business owners, managers as well as new business owners to get their view on this. Four key reasons were revealed. Firstly, it is evident that many owner/managers have no desire to develop, being content to limit the scope of the business to suit their lifestyle; the majority of these are family owned businesses. Secondly, others simply do not have the knowledge, skills or aptitude to develop their businesses. Thirdly, some are limited in personal financial resources and are unable to persuade others to assist them financially. Then lastly, there are those owners who have the desire to develop but simply have poor judgment, recruiting the wrong people, taking the wrong advice and following strategies which have low probabilities of success. The most common trait of all the four categories is the entrepreneur or manager who wants to be involved in every decision and every activity of the business. Clearly most entrepreneurs fail not because they are not talented or because they have no internal value or vision but because they lack external support.

> *"A dream you dream alone is only a dream. A dream you dream together is reality."*
> *John Lennon*

Have you ever paid attention to the geese when they fly? They usually fly in a "V" formation. By flying in V formation, the whole flock increases the flight performance by 71% compared to just one bird on its own. When you are connected with people who share common direction and purpose, your journey becomes quicker and faster. When a goose falls out of formation, it suddenly feels the drag and resistance of trying to go it alone – and quickly gets back into formation to take advantage of the lifting power of the bird in front.

If you have as much sense as a goose, you will stay in formation with those people who are headed the same way you are. When the head goose gets tired, it rotates back in the wing and another goose flies point. It is sensible to take turns sharing the hardest tasks and problems. It is the same whether with people or with geese flying south. Geese honk from behind to encourage those up front to keep up their speed. Finally, and this is important, when a goose gets sick or is wounded by gunshot, and falls out of formation, two other geese fall out with that goose and follow it down to lend help and protection. They stay with the fallen goose until it is able to fly or until it dies: and only then do they launch out on their own, or with another formation to catch up with their group.

Highly successful people have resilience. If you have been in business for longer you will know that business plans do not usually go as written because they are often based on numerous assumptions. Hence when it comes to implementation, a lot of factors which are beyond your control will begin to unravel. Thus the business may not develop in the manner originally planned. Experience shows that the best solution to this problem is to have a proven network of people who have the experience to cope with the changes which inevitably will occur.

No one gets to the top of their game alone. You need to have the right people on the team to get there. This team could be your employees, business partners, advisors, peer groups or even be your parents. You need to realize that your vision is connected to other people's vision. Especially when you are starting out, the take off becomes easier when you have the support which gives you the stability.

There is a growing body of research which shows that highly successful businesses are started by individuals who are extremely talented. These individuals have extensive networks which enables them to recruit the right employees and are able to establish strategic partnerships with their networks. With their networks, they have access to contracts with established suppliers and open doors to key customer accounts.

Let us look at one of the pioneers of software revolution – Steve Jobs. He showed an early interest in electronics and gadgetry. Steve called Bill Hewlett (Hewlett-Packard co-founder) to ask for parts for a school project. Impressed by Jobs, Hewlett not only gave him the parts, but also offered him a summer internship at Hewlett-Packard. While at Hewlett-Packard, Jobs met and befriended Steve Wozniak, a young engineer five years his senior who later co-founded Apple with Jobs.

Was Jobs not talented, did he not have access to networks of organisation? Was he not able to recruit the right candidate? Highly successful people recognize that there are many things that other people are a lot better at doing than they are. The ability to realize this and getting the right people multiplies your efforts and results such that you become more productive and hence wealthier, I earn to focus one thing you are exceptionally good at and what you most enjoy (even if it is just dreaming up new ideas).

When you are connected with the right people, your vision becomes stronger, you have a sense of partnership and a personal achievement which gives you the capability to grow and take advantage of opportunities in the market place. Through your networks, you will have access to new ideas, be willing to try new approaches to doing business and encouraged to take bold risks which will proactively generate avenues for growth.

As you know, the entrepreneurial journey can be lonely; who do you turn to when you have issues? Who do you run your ideas by?

Bruce D. Johnson, President and Founder of Wired To Grow, concluded that there are at least seven 'types' of people you need in your life. Note that one person can also wear multiple hats.

So, here are the seven types:

1. **An Encourager.** Every leader needs at least one person who is always on their side. One person they can turn to and know; 'not only does this person have my back,

but they'll find the positive in whatever I'm dealing with. They won't critique me. They won't give me a hard time. They'll just support me and say that whatever I'm doing is right.' Sometimes this person is internal to your business or organization. They can be a key team player, an administrative assistant or someone who's been around for a long time. But often, they're someone outside of your organization who you know you can call up at any time and they'll lift your spirits and breathe new life into you. So, who is your encourager?

2. **A "Yes, But" Person**. While most of us as leaders don't like this person a whole lot—you know, the person who always seems to be an 'Eeyore', who always sees the negative, who always sees what could go wrong—the reality is that we need this person on the team. Yes, we have to work with them to not always see the negative but the reality is that every one of us can be biased in perception which means that there are things we ought to see before making a decision which we just don't. And that is why we all need a "yes, but" person in our lives (as painful as that is) because they actually make us better decision-makers. So, who is your "Yes, but" person? Keep them close

3. **A Core Teammate**. Every leader, as he or she builds out their team, needs to find at least one person (occasionally two) who really gets them. Even though Steve Jobs had a great top team, it was Jony Ivy who

was his core teammate. Or during Jack Welch's reign at GE, it was his HR guy, Bill Conaty who served in that role. Yes, you want to build a talented team at the top. And yes, everyone is valuable. But you also need to find that one person who really gets you. Who makes you "a better man" (if you like movie quotes). You need that one person who day in and day out helps you get things done at a higher level, who thinks like you think and who operates like your "right hand." So, who's your core teammate?

4. **A Confidante.** Rarely is this person someone inside your organization (unless you're a fan of the Godfather) because every leader needs someone they can turn to and talk with—and not have to worry about the repercussions of that conversation. In light of that, my experience has been that the best person for this key role isn't a staff member or board member—or even a spouse (if you're married). Instead, you want to look for someone outside your business who's a trusted friend or advisor, whose advice you respect and who you know will never divulge the content of your conversations. It's that perfect combination of wisdom, the ability to ask good questions, listen intently and keep confidences that makes this person so valuable to you. So, who is your confidante?

5. **A Coach.** Every business leader needs a coach, period. To get to the next level, you need a coach.

Someone outside of your circle who will help you see things you can't see, fill in parts you don't get and who will push you when you need to be pushed. This is why all great athletes and all great business leaders have them. Bottom line, coaches make all of us better. So, who's your coach?

6. **A Mentor.** The difference between mentors and coaches is usually related to cost (mentors are frequently free, coaches are paid). The randomness of meetings, (coaching meetings typically happen on a regular schedule like every other week vs. mentoring which tends to be sporadic–when a need arises), and the lack of accountability (i.e. mentors are rarely checking up and seeing what progress you've made vs. coaches are). Mentors can be board members (if you have a board) but usually they're people who have gone a level or two (or more) beyond you and who are willing to offer advice on an 'as needed' basis. While you might schedule a monthly or quarterly meeting with them, mostly what you want is someone who's seasoned, who possesses **IP** that you don't, and who is willing to take your call (or email) when it comes in. So, who is your mentor?

7. **An Accountability Partner.** The seventh and final person that every leader needs in their life is an accountability partner. This is critical for you as a business leader because, while you may hold others accountable, rarely

will anyone else hold you accountable for your decisions and actions. For example, rarely will an employee say to the owner of a company, "Hey, you said you were going to get X done by Y date. That date has passed. What happened?" Which is why you need someone else in your life to do that for you? You need someone who won't be afraid of you and won't be afraid to ask the hard questions. You need an accountability partner. So, who is your accountability partner?

Looking at these seven types, how are you doing? Do you have all seven types? Do you have someone who wears multiple hats for you—maybe a coach who is also your confidante and your accountability partner? If you're missing anyone of these people, make a commitment to find them over the next month or so. And if you have at least one person in each category, why not expand the circle? In as much as you are reading this book, you have fulfilled part of your connection so why don't you go and find the remaining team? You really don't have to go far; they are just waiting to be unleashed.

CHAPTER EIGHT

THE LAW OF GROWTH

"Growth is never by mere chance; it is the result of forces working together."

- James Cash Penney, Founder of JCPenney

Every Sunday morning while getting ready for church, my parents will normally give us money to put in the offering basket in church. As children, we were taught that when you give money to God (in church), you are sowing and you will harvest later. Although the prosperity message was not popular then as it is now, we believed a coin could do the miracle. Since then I had the mindset that money is a seed and whatever is not your harvest is definitely a seed. So I keep sowing. As I continue to grow and learn, I realised money is not just the only seed, there are other seeds and if they are seeds, apparently they are worth sowing if you want them to grow. So what are these seeds? How do you grow them to guarantee your harvest?

Let us look at what the law of growth states. Quite simply the law of growth states that for every seed planted a harvest will be received. That means the law Of growth can only ensure a harvest the same in kind and quality as the seeds planted. So for there to be growth, three conditions must be met:

(1) There must be a Seed(s),
(2) All the seeds must be of the same kind and quality,
(3) They must be planted.

Once these conditions are met, the law of growth in its absolute perfect timing guarantees a 100% certainty combined with the unfailing interconnected certainty of all other laws mentioned. That means a bountiful harvest is inevitable. As any farmer knows, the growth of a crop only happens when the right ingredients are present. To harvest plentiful fields, the farmer has to begin by planting the right seed in rich topsoil where sunlight and water can help the seed to sprout, mature and bear fruit. If any of the ingredients (quality seeds, topsoil, sunlight, or water) are missing, the crop won't grow.

Having a proper understanding of how this law pertains to your success is essential because it will enable you to be consciously aware of the seeds that you are planting which will determine your harvest. Growing as an entrepreneur or a professional also requires the proper ingredients. We have established that we all have internal value which can be exchanged for money. Let us take your internal value to be the seed. That means for this seed to continue to grow and bring harvest, it must meet the conditions mentioned.

If you were like me some years ago with the mindset that money is the only seed one can sow, you need to repent now. Maybe you don't even consider money to be a seed, well if the few words in this book are not able to convince you then I recommend you carry out a specific research. Ignorance is no excuse. I learned that the valuable seeds in life are what the physical eyes cannot see. They are numerous in number, unquantifiable and priceless. They are love, joy, peace, happiness, forgiveness, kindness, nurturing, prayers, commitment, loyalty, friendship, hard work, dedication, diligence, patience, endurance, empathy, sympathy; the list is endless. These invaluable seeds are what I considered as the ingredients that will enhance the quality of your seed.

"Without continual growth and progress, such words as improvement, achievement and success have no meaning." - Benjamin Franklin

Let us take for instance that you have a great idea that can generate millions of dollars. If you are not committed to the project , it will continue to remain an idea. If you are an employee and you are not diligent in your work, how can you be successful in your career? If you have money and don't have peace, how can you enjoy your life? All these ingredients ensure that your seed is of a good quality so that when planted it will automatically bring bountiful harvest. There are many examples that you can think of to help you understand this such as the quality of an egg to fertilize into a new life.

While this chapter is not focusing on these ingredients, it is worth mentioning so that you understand that these ingredients are essentially important to the quality of your seed. It is not possible to list all the seeds that you can grow but for the purpose of this book, I have highlighted five key areas I recommend you to focus on growing. Once you succeed in ensuring the seed planted in this area are of good quality and planted, you will be sure of a bountiful harvest. The areas you need to grow are, your thoughts, your personal life, your business, your money and your relationship with people.

So how do you grow these five areas;

1. **Grow Your Thoughts.** Your thoughts are a seed and therefore they must be of good quality. They must be planted and nurtured and will definitely bring forth100% of its kind. Here is a paragraph from the book *As a Man Thinketh by James Allen.* "A man's mind may be likened to a garden, which may be intelligently cultivated or allowed to run wild. But whether cultivated or neglected, it must and will, bring forth. If no useful seeds are put into it, then an abundance of useless weed seeds will fall therein and will continue to produce their kind."

   Another way to look at being successful is viewing it as a change of thought causing a shift in the way you perceive things. Simply changing your thought will cause a rearranging of your cognitive behaviour and definitely affect the way you do things. Let us see how that works historically. Thousands of years ago, people were used to journeying thousands of miles on foot. Only the rich could afford donkeys or camels. This was a dangerous and unpredictable way to live. The desire to have more stability and safety caused human beings to think. Eventually, there came ships, railroad, cars etc. The idea simply changed the way people see themselves. Everything thing changed and created an avenue for further development. What are your thoughts concerning your life, your business and your community? So the next time the thought of hatred towards someone comes, you weed it away because it is a seed and it will grow. The harvest is definitely not pleasant.

2. **Grow Your Personal Life**. I have had the privilege of working with a number of business owners and senior executives as they grow their business .Very often a business will reach a certain level and then plateau. Even with so much struggle, they can't seem to get past the ceiling. These plateaus occur for many reasons but the most common cause is personal growth. When you cannot see where you are going personally, you undermine the opportunities you provide for everyone else to grow including your business. In

growing your personal life there are three most important areas you need to focus on and these are your health, your relationship and your personal development. Once you accept the responsibility to develop your personal life, consciously and subconsciously, your thoughts and actions will direct their energy to making it happen. Once you have a quality personal life, it will also affect your thought life. I suggest you examine your personal life within the next month and have an action plan in place to increase the quality. Reading this book is a way of improving the quality of your life.

3. **Grow Your Business**. In most societies throughout the world, growth in business is often equated with progress and success. While growth is recognised as inevitable, not all successful people view the process or the philosophy behind growth in the same way. No matter how good your business idea or concept is, without an intention to grow, or how growth objectives can be achieved, the business might not go pass the four corners of your room. There are many possible ways an entrepreneur can grow his business but you will need to choose those which are most appropriate for the type of product or service you are offering as well as the preferences of your target customer. At the start of your business, one key question you need to

consider is: when your business is generating income, what position will you hold in the business? Some people can only manage a small business, when the business grows and becomes complex, they could become lost in the process. The business no longer becomes fun. You need to bear in mind that your business has the capacity to grow ten times than what you initially had but when it does, how will that impact your life? What are your growth plans to increase your distribution channels? What are your plans to grow the capability of your business when its generating income?

4. **Grow Your Money**. Money is a seed. It is the most talked about seed by all. A major key to building lasting wealth is in planting your money by investing it so that it works for you, instead of you working for your money. When you take a portion of your income from each day and put it into investments that grow on their own, automatically and without any further work, over a long-term period they will grow. That way, a portion of each day that you work for money ends up working back for you for many years to come. That is a major key to growing wealth; getting a percentage of your income every day to work back for you without your intervention. There are many investments you can use, from stocks, mutual funds, certain types of bank accounts that have high and above-inflation interest

rates, real estate investment bonds, etc.

When you plant your money in the right investment, you are not required to do anything. You simply invest, walk away and your money grows all on its own. Even one dollar can turn into a million dollars in a certain amount of years at a certain compound interest rate. One dollar, just one dollar, can grow into a million dollars all on its own without your intervention. You would be pleasantly surprised to know that a single dollar placed into an investment that grows at 20 percent a year will become $1 million in seventy-five years. That is just one dollar! All you would need to do is leave it alone, go away, go to sleep for seventy-five years, just leave it alone. When you return it will be $1 million without any effort from you, other than the fact that you placed that single dollar somewhere! Now, if in addition to the initial one dollar you put in a dollar every single day into the same 20-percent-a-year growth investment, you would end up with $1 million in thirty-two years instead of seventy-five. In fact, a dollar a day would become $1 billion in sixty-six years. A higher interest rate would dramatically shorten that time. This shows you that you can never have too little to start with. Whatever your income today, discipline yourself into the habit of investing 10 percent of your income before you pay bills or taxes or anything else. Put aside a percentage for investing in well-selected investments consistently.

Consistency is the key. Compound interest will always work for you without asking anything from you. Your only part is to be consistent to choose good investments and to stay put. Invest your money in buying more assets than liabilities. In as much as good cars are lovely to possess, they are liabilities. Houses on mortgages are liabilities to you but assets to the bank. There is nothing wrong with having those lovely cars and other liabilities, just ensure that your assets are more than your liabilities.

5. **Grow People.** We have established that your vision is connected to others and that everyone in your life is for a purpose and all have roles to play in fulfilling your dream. How do you help other people to grow without seeing them as a threat? How do you grow your staff if you are undermining them? To truly grow people, you need to give them a chance to develop and express their creativity. They may be able to see areas where the business can be more successful and they may come up with some creative suggestions. It will also give them the opportunity to have a chance to voice their own concerns and could help to shape the business in such a way that is acceptable to all parties. Apart from developing your team, you need to be

committed to developing your community by either mentoring people or sponsoring them. The roles of sponsors and mentors are similar but the objectives are different. A mentor is a person or a friend who guides a less experienced person by building trust and modelling positive behaviours whilst a Sponsor helps through the provision of products or services. You can wear both hats but the bottom-line is, sow a seed of greatness in somebody and it might be the greatest and most rewarding investment you would ever make.

CHAPTER NINE

THE LAW OF PROCESS

"Life is a process of becoming, a combination of states we have to go through. Where people fail is that they wish to elect a state and remain in it. This is a kind of death".

- Anais Nin

I enjoy microwave instant noodle and particularly like the fact that it is ready about 2-3 minutes from when I decided I wanted one. I am also amazed at how technology has changed and become faster and faster over the years. But my favourite is that when I decide I want to speak on the phone with someone, I can connect with them in less than 10 seconds from the moment I made the decision. The experience above is not uncommon and in most cases, we have come to expect that when we want something, that means we want it now! When it is not happening within 2-3minutes like the instant noodle, we are likely to be really frustrated - it would seem to be forever.

As a society, we have developed an expectation of "instant" or "microwave results" and if those results are not met within the time frame we have established in our minds, then we tend to get frustrated, and maybe quit working towards a successful outcome. Having dreams and visions is healthy. It gives us purpose and a way to evolve and grow. It doesn't matter how large or small these dreams and visions are, they are the motivation and passion that ignites a flame inside your heart. It doesn't matter what the dreams are, they are what you desire to achieve. The biggest error people make is focusing on result. When we do this we tend to want instant gratification and look for short cuts to get there. What happens when we take short cuts is that we can often get lost or fail.

Are you familiar with any of these adverts?
"Get rich in 7 days"
 "Lose 30 lbs of fat in 15 days"

"Find your soul mate in 7 days"

When people subscribe to things like the above, research shows that their state becomes worse if their expectations are not met. Those of you who have tried to lose weight with quick diets will know what I mean. They will seem like they are working and may even give you results for a short period of time and then before long you have gained the weight back and some more. Professionals have been telling us that weight loss comes with consistent and long-term lifestyle changes. A healthy diet and regular exercise is the best way to lose weight and keep it off. Those of us in small businesses know by experience that it is very rare to have instant success and that it is in the process of taking one step at a time that we build our success. Business coaches, speakers and other professionals will all agree that success comes after a process of time.

Do you think that the inventor of microwave technology developed it in 15 seconds? No, it was likely 2-3 years and guess what, they are still perfecting their successes. These days, what seems like "instant" or "microwave success" is becoming an expectation for almost everything, usually because the people observing the success of others do not know about the actual amount of work the person has done before they got there. Those who are successful were just ready to receive success and that is when it came to them, but they became ready by being a student of The Law of Process.

The manufacturing industry defines the process time as, "The period during which one or more inputs are transformed into a finished product by a manufacturing procedure". This means there is a set period for all 'finished products' to be transformed. Did you notice the word 'finished'? Does that mean there are unfinished products? Could it be that the unfinished product did not complete their life cycle –process?

Are we right to say everything becomes a finished product in the course of time or as time goes on, gradually, in due course, etc? Which means the end of a specific period of time that has been specifically set aside in the procedure. It is important that you do not misconstrue process with timing. Timing is the point when you decide to take action; it is when you make the decision to do something. That is what we mean by taking advantage of time. The law of process explains that, success does not occur by chance, instantly or in the microwave; success goes through transformation within a set period.

"The system is that there is no system. That doesn't mean we don't have process. Apple is a very disciplined company and we have great processes. But that's not what it's about. Process makes you more efficient".

- Steve Jobs

Our society has always recognised exceptional individuals whose achievements are vastly superior to that of the rest of the population. Sometimes when we read their stories it sounds as if it happened in an instant or that what they did was so simple. As simple as it might seem, we fail to realise that it took a lot of input and resources to come to that simple task that brought about outstanding results. There are also speculations that the causes of these individuals' extraordinary abilities and achievements are as a result divine intervention, genetically transmitted or having some kind of environmental factors. Whichever of the above might be responsible for such outstanding results could not have occurred over night. Things are acquired slowly, patiently over a very long time as a result of hard work, consistency, practice, giving and so on. You can refer to these as the ingredients your seed required for growth, as discussed in the previous chapter.

You know that growth is not static, from the point that a farmer plants his seed to the time of harvest are different stages and these can be referred to as the farming process. You need to understand that just like the farmer, when you have a quality idea, plant it with the right ingredients but it has to go through a period of transformation before it becomes a finished product. Many researchers have come up with different theories that suggest the process it takes an individual to achieve outstanding results. The most common is the deliberate practice which uses the 10,000 hour/10 year rule. Three hugely successful books in particular were published between 2008 and 2009 that used deliberate practice as their foundation for explaining how to develop expertise across domains: Outliers (Gladwell, 2008), Talent is Overrated (Colvin, 2008) and The Talent Code (Coyle, 2009).

The "10,000-Hour Rule", according to Gladwell, claims that the key to success in any field is, to a large extent, a matter of practicing a specific task for a total of around 10,000 hours. He used The Beatles and Bill Gates as examples stating: "The Beatles performed live in Hamburg, Germany over 1,200 times from 1960 to 1964, amassing more than 10,000 hours of playing time. Therefore meeting the 10,000-Hour Rule, Gladwell asserts that all of the time The Beatles spent performing shaped their talent and quotes Beatles' biographer Philip Norman as saying, "So by the time they returned to England from Hamburg, Germany, 'they sounded like no one else. It was the making of them". Gates met the 10,000-Hour Rule when he gained access to a high school computer in 1968 at the age of 13, and spent 10,000 hours programming on it.

You can disagree with Gladwell if you wish but the bottom line is that every outstanding achievement underwent a structured process. I have met with some individuals who had to terminate their professional careers or businesses for reasons unrelated to their ability to perform. Once they could no longer commit sufficient time and energy required to complete the process life cycle, they stopped the business completely because they could not accept performing at a lower level. The problem is, most of the time they compare themselves to their peer in business or career that have outstanding results but they failed to investigate how long it took them to achieve such results. Many researchers found out that individuals with outstanding performance in sports or music start out as children by engaging in playful activities in their domain. After a period of playful and enjoyable experiences, they reveal "talent" or promise. At this point their parents typically suggest the start of instruction by a teacher. Their increased experience and outstanding performance is found to be associated with the amounts of constant daily practice over extended periods of time.

While slow success is no one's best ally, focusing on the result alone is also frustrating. Tools like the vision board has been prescribed in the bid to get people motivated to achieve their goals. The vision board was also criticised for giving a false sense of achievement and that action board helps individual focus on the process (doing) than the results (achievement).

Understanding the law of process connects you to the ingredients (internal value) of patience and persistence and helps you to break things down into small, manageable steps that take you closer to your vision and dreams. Imagine a farmer who plants a seed, the seed germinates after few days or weeks (depending on the plant), when the plant begins to grow, he does not jump straight to harvest. He waits for the buds to appear, then fruits and the fruits become ripen for harvest. Trying to take the short cut will only result in nothing but failure.

What is it that you want to achieve? Understand that it will require 'process' for you to achieve your desired result. Learn from Thomas Edison not to give up even though it may take you 10,000 attempts to achieve it. Outstanding success is achievable, but it requires a process.

Here are three exercises that can help you:

1. **Meditate.** Create a quiet time for meditation, it can be fifteen or so minutes a day. Find a protected space — bathtub, bedroom, local trail, coffee shop —-that works for you for your meditation time. I have found out that the bathtub works for me irrespective of the time of the day and also observing a quiet time very early in the morning has helped me to prepare for the day and evaluate myself. You can call this a time of reflection; it helps you to examine your life and get rid of the toxic residue from our life experiences into something we can work with, something that is not harmful to harbour within. Learning how to do this well will help you turn resentment into peace, disappointment into understanding, wounds into healing, and confusion into clarity. Imagine a farmer removing the weeds and turning them to manure. Don't confuse the weed to be plants, get rid of them and have a clear focus of your field.

2. **Create Systems in Your Business.** Everything is a system. How you think and approach a problem is a system. How you go about creating something is a system. How you try to sell something is a system. How you lead a team or recruit an employee is a system. Everything you do is a system. The downside to not

creating systems is that, not only do you get frustrated but you also achieve less especially if you are an entrepreneur and you have employees. My experience has been that most employees actually want to do their jobs well. However, when it is not clear what they are supposed to do or how they are supposed to do it, etc. then they get frustrated as well. In which case you are frustrated that they are not getting their job done and they are frustrated that you have not clearly communicated to them what your expectations are, as well as how they should do what you want them to do. Have you asked yourself, what do you do when a key employee gets sick? Or goes on vacation? Or takes another job? Or worse still, dies suddenly? What do you do then? If all of their intellectual property is left in their head, you're in massive trouble. The problem is that by not creating systems, you have to work a whole lot harder and longer. The good news is that as soon as you start creating systems for everything your business does, you will be taking steps toward having a life again. Why? Because you won't be as needed by your employees all the time. And when you're no longer needed for the day-to-day operations of your business (meaning others have to take over virtually all of the tasks that need to be completed daily), you'll be able to focus your attention on what is needed for the future— which will allow you to grow your business faster and more profitably. And the journey becomes more enjoyable.

3. **Mastermind with Other Leaders.** Have mentors and a coach; people who are having success in the area you want to succeed in; people who are willing to teach you and keep you on track. Once you get a hold of them, do not let go! If you let them get away, they will not wait for you to catch up.

You have probably heard a thousand times that the journey is just as important as the destination. It is because it is in the journey that we grow and evolve and makes us who we are and the destination is just the prize. So enjoy your journey!

CHAPTER TEN

THE LAW OF CREATIVITY

"I never made one of my discoveries through the process of rational thinking"

- Albert Einstein

Contrary to some people's view, creativity is not solely pertaining to those within the so-called creative industries such as theatre, arts, design, journalism and the media at large. This is far, far too narrow a view. Creativity is the force which resides in you, unique to you, that wants to be expressed. It is the ability to solve problems, tackle issues, grasp opportunities and indeed, create opportunities to come up with fresh, exciting, value-adding solutions. Each of your daily activities should be considered as an act of creation. It is not only about great works of art. To know the law of creativity, means, simply, that you will know how best to express yourself.

For an entrepreneur, it can be applied to the processes of identifying new ideas of products or services, different ways of delivering value to your clients, new ways to differentiate your business from others, and new ways by which your teams can reach an even higher level of performance as well as the formulation of a new and distinctive strategy.

In this light, creativity is clearly a requirement for truly successful businesses. Because underpinning all of these challenges and opportunities is a single, unifying concept: Introducing a new service, delivering services in new ways, doing pricing differently, differentiating your business in the market, determining a unique strategy that really differentiates—these can only be done *if you have an idea first* and not just any idea, but a quality one.

If you have been observing, you will notice the interconnectivity of these laws from chapter one – the law of reflection. You can have one without desiring the other but they work hand in hand, so that when mastered, will surely guarantee success. What the law of creativity does to your seed (internal value), is to multiply it into different forms. Sometimes the same seed can produce a different product in another form and can sometimes deliver different values. So how does creativity happen? What do you have to do or be to make it happen? When does it happen?

"If I had asked people what they wanted, they'd have said faster horses."

- Henry Ford

Firstly you don't have to be a creative person to make it happen, just being a person who possess a brain is all that you need to be. Certainly, we have all had that wonderful experience of a great idea just coming "out of the blue." But relying on a magical moment as the only process for creativity is tremendously weak. It is more sensible to adopt a process that is deliberate and systematic.

"Don't be a solution provider, be part of the creative force"
(quote)

The big question, of course, is: How? How can we use our brains in a deliberate and systematic way, to generate ideas on demand?

The four points below will help you to answer that question:

1. **Change from a Competitive Mindset**. No one is going to "take your share" or "beat you to it." There is more than enough for everyone. The only time there is not enough, the only time when you are "beaten to it" is when you think and act competitively. Instead, start thinking and acting creatively, trusting that in the process of time, your seed will germinate and you will receive a bountiful harvest. Thinking and acting competitively makes it harder for you to patiently and cheerfully wait for your time of harvest. It brings about frustration and if not careful, you start running someone else's race. Thinking creatively and non-competitively helps you be in agreement with all your ingredients of growth which are the requirements for extraordinary results.

2. **Change from a Scarcity Mindset**. Sometime ago, I thought that creativity was all about inventing something

"brand-new. I later realised that this belief is entirely wrong. Creativity is not about the 'brand new', for the 'brand-new' in essence, does not exist. Let us consider music. Neither Beethoven nor the Beatles "invented" musical notes. When they composed their music, the notes were already there. What they did and what every composer who has ever lived has done, was to craft *patterns* of these already-existing notes. Not just any old patterns, but rather beautiful patterns, according to their subjective view of beauty. A scarcity mindset gives you a false belief that what you require to be creative does not exist. Remember the law that says energy is neither created nor destroyed, it only changes form? The musical note did not drop from the heavens, they simply changed their thought pattern and it was done. Let us look at another example; The Sony Walkman, the blockbuster consumer product of the late 20th century, first launched in 1979. Sony Walkman is a "pattern" formed from electronic components that play back (but don't record), a cassette tape and headphones. Miniaturised electronic components evolved with the first transistor radios, which date back to the mid-1950s. The electronics company Philips introduced the compact cassette in 1963 and headphones had been around for a century. Sony was simply the first organisation to form the pattern of the Walkman from components that already existed none of which were invented by Sony. There is no scarcity, it only exists in your brain.

3. **Desire a Better Life** through a desire to make something good even better. Today, the desire to trade even faster has caused us to have currency markets and stock exchanges. Imagine the time when a trader had to walk for half a day to the market, sell one cow and then walk back home for half a day. Next came trucks and farmers could drive several cows to the market and be back home early enough to do another trip. Then came futures and options exchanges, which enabled people to buy and sell thousands of livestock futures and options in seconds without having to get up or move a single cow! Yet nothing dropped from the heavens. It was all right here. People just desired to have a better life.

    Today, life is different. We are born assuming, from observation, that a house is something that we shall automatically always live in, and that we shall automatically have cloths and certain other things that were reserved for royalty back then. It does not even cross your mind for a moment that you can lack certain things, yet people in the past struggled for generations to get those same things.

    Take for example the emergence of the IT boom. You had Bill Gates and hundreds of other young people making massive amounts of wealth in very short periods of time. Today, people can become billionaires in a few years instead of four generations as it used to take. And as fresh kids out of college watched this happen, they believed they could do it. And many of them believed. And a whole range of new businesses were formed in no time at all. Young people in their twenties were becoming millionaires by the dozens every day and yet nothing new dropped from the heavens in those few years. All it took was massive desire, belief and change of thought.

And just as millions of people today live better than a few kings lived in the past, the very near future will have billions of average people living better than millionaires live today. And nothing new will be dropped from the heavens. We will simply desire better because we are now beginning to understand how it all works, and we will change our thoughts the right way, and it will just happen.

4. **Ask questions.** We all see the world differently and we all notice different things even when we are looking at the same thing; our description will be different. In every situation, seek other people's views; ask questions, "How might this be different?" This is where you generate ideas, because it is in this process that you discover different patterns by bringing your experience of *other components* to bear on the problem of interest. And when you feel you have explored one idea sufficiently, you choose another, and then another, and then another. And the ideas just keep flowing.

From a business perspective, no business can achieve extraordinary results on the back of a single creativity. Generally it requires a process of continual creativity over a longer period of time. It has to be a way of life, a systematic process that you consciously inject into your system. Now that you have the full set of creation tools with you, let us look at the fuel that makes them work. They need one major ingredient to work. The Ingredient is so powerful that no other force can equal it . . . you will discover this in the next chapter so read on.

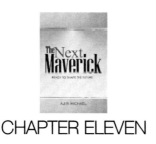

CHAPTER ELEVEN

THE LAW OF FAITH

"Faith is the external elixir which gives life, power and action to the impulse thought! Faith is the starting point of all accumulation of riches! Faith is the basis of all miracles and all mysteries which cannot be analyzed by the rules of science! Faith is the only known antidote for failure!"

-Napoleon Hill

No matter where the ultimate destination might be, the ability to determine the course is the most essential element needed for achieving our dreams. Effort without direction may not amount to anything of value. 'So where are we going?' You may ask. That is what all followers want to know. This is what leaders pretend to be sure of. The reality is that most people who walk by faith have difficulty answering that one dreadful question. They have difficulty because faith is an abstract and the question is asking for a concrete answer.

Faith is intangible; it can't be articulated and can't be explained. It is something that just is.

Faith is that thing, that place, that indescribable something that we pursue without fully being able to explain to others the unique drive we have towards it. It is that inner feeling, that "Yes, I am looking for something. There is something in here for me. I do not know exactly what it is but when I see it, I will know it." How will you know? Quite honestly, I am not sure. All I know is that when it is in front of me, I will know that this is it. In essence, what I am saying is that there is a compass in our souls that inform us inwardly when it is the right man, the right woman, or whatever it is we pursue.

Across many walks of life, one thing that highly successful people have in common is that they know. If you read about the stories of huge, successful entrepreneurs you will find a few commonalities, namely that they all had an unwavering belief in themselves. Bill Gates dropped out of Harvard because he knew he'd be successful in life and that it was time for him to join the business world. John Lennon, one of the greatest influencers of music in our time and Steven Tyler both say that they knew they were great musicians before anyone else did. Sam Walten believed in himself and what he was creating even when he was 2 million dollars in debt and trying to get Walmart off the ground.

"If you can? Everything is possible for him who believes".

-Jesus Christ

This is a pretty cool picture and a good reminder that you don't have to see the whole staircase... sometimes you just have to step out in faith and go for it! Each step you take reveals the next step. But we all know the first step is the hardest. It often requires that you break out of your comfort zone and overcome the inertia of standing still. The good news is... inertia works both ways. Yes, It is hard to get going but once you create that initial momentum, the effort to keep going gets easier and easier.

Think about best-selling authors... earning a spot on the best-seller list is hard. But once they earn the label "best-selling author," subsequent best-sellers seem to come much easier. James Patterson is a great example. His first manuscript was rejected over 30 times! Now it seems he has a new best-seller every week! But when Patterson submitted his first manuscript, he had no idea that he would become one of the most commercially successful fiction writers of all-time. But it wouldn't have happened had he not taken that first step. As the "perfect moment" rarely presents itself, if you spend your life waiting for everything to line up just right, then you may be waiting a long time!

I hope I have been able to describe what faith means, enough to propel you into action. No matter the vision you have, the quality of your seed, even if you apply all the laws mentioned in the previous chapter and you don't have faith, your probability of success is very weak.

You might be thinking that faith is a religious thing but I can assure you everyone needs it. It is not restricted to any religion, house or race. It is not contained in the museum, in the glass, moon, roses and crosses. It is a strong unsinkable determination to bring about a change. It is in the hearts, spirit, soul and body of men and women who are called to be the mothers of invisible dreams and the fathers of feats unbelievable to other people. Whenever you see real, raw unpretentious faith in anybody, watch them; they are giant killers, mountain movers and life changers. They know the equation. These are the people who will lead the way in the twenty-first century. With faith, they can go to that "place" they have not been.

"Take the first step in faith. You don't have to see the whole staircase, just take the first step".
-Martin Luther King, Jr.

There are so many books written on faith, and they all give you different illustrations. Why? Because faith is indescribable. It is within and no one can have faith for you. Your business advisor can help you map out a plan for your business but cannot have faith for you. Faith is personal, it is within. It is "Do It Your Self."

Below are two key exercises that can help boost your faith:

1. **Set goals.** Goal setting is one of the most important, yet difficult steps toward achieving success. Goals give you clarity and a sense of direction. They lift the fog and give you a feeling of control over your life instead of

drifting aimlessly from one day to the next, like a sail boat without sails. Goals empower you and bridge the gap between where you are and where you want to be. But setting goals is one of the hardest things most people face. It is not difficult once you get started, but getting started is where most people fail. The most successful people on the planet are intensely goal-driven. So if you want to be successful, doesn't it make sense to model your actions after theirs?

It may be difficult to think about where you want to be in 5 years, or 10 years but the key is to get moving. Just create some forward momentum and use the power of inertia to your advantage. You may have to take a job that is less than ideal but it doesn't have to last forever. Look at it as a stepping stone on your path to discovering your true destiny.

It's been said that we can't go back and create a new beginning but we can start today and create a new ending and goals are the key to making this happen. Look inside yourself and ask what things and activities inspire you. These are the building blocks for an exciting and successful future.

You don't have to know exactly where you're going to end up. Just follow your passion and when the time is right, everything will click into place. This is the formula for success that has been used by top achievers since the beginning of time.

2. **Be Persistent**. Persistence breeds faith. You can use persistence to increase your faith. And through faith, you have persistence. By persisting, even when it looks like you should give up, you can increase your faith in an outcome and bring it about.

   The question is, Do you have faith in yourself? Do you have faith in your dreams? Do you have faith in the plans you laid out for achieving your dreams? The answer to these questions will determine what happens in the next chapter.

CHAPTER TWELVE

THE LAW OF REWARD

"The purpose here is to reward yourself for a job well done. This is positive reinforcement. The reward is an opportunity to stop and smell the roses that bloom as a result of your hard work."

— K. Jeffrey Miller

Over the last few years, I've been driving myself hard with achieving various goals — from waking early to meditate, running round the block, to eliminating my debt and more. And what I have learned has repeatedly taught me that the principal fuel for achieving your goals is reward – that is all you need. I realised that the more I reward myself, the more goals I am able to achieve and the nearer I get to my dreams.

Some people tell me they motivate themselves in order to achieve their goals. When I ask them how, they can't explain. Sometimes I hear things like, "accomplishing my goals is enough to motivate me." While I agree that accomplishing your goals can motivate, it is totally different from reward. That form of motivation is intangible while reward is tangible. You can motivate yourself to do something you don't like to do. But if you really don't enjoy it, you'll only be able to keep it up for so long. And even if you could do it for months and years is that something you would want to do? If you don't enjoy it, why do it at all. But, you might say, 'what if it's something I really want to achieve but I don't enjoy it?' My question is, why do something you don't enjoy? That is self inflicting punishment! What reward does for you is that it helps you identify ways to find enjoyment in most things — the key is to focus on the enjoyable parts. Focus on the reward.

A lot of people have told me how they have problems achieving their goals and have said they simply lack the discipline to stick with things for very long. But discipline is also different from reward because people use discipline to get things done for fear of being reprimanded, yet they don't get a sense of satisfaction doing it. Imagine an employee working longer hours to complete a project, that does not mean he derives satisfaction from it; he/she knows they will get told off or punished if the deadline is not met.

There are so many entrepreneurs today who work so hard for long hours and believe you just save and save some more and live a frugal lifestyle and make sacrifices financially. If you are one these people, I say to you, just get ready to stop the madness. Without mincing words, it is so important to reward yourself. Rewarding yourself actually helps you to prosper even more. Yes, it is important to definitely live below your means but it is also vital to have a way of celebrating each goal attained that actually helps emphasise and confirm that you are doing a good job and that you are on the right track.

It has been proven that when people feel better about themselves in performing and accomplishing certain tasks, they will be motivated and enthusiastic to continue doing them. We mentioned in the previous chapter about setting smaller goals as a faith booster, so when you achieve one goal, reward yourself, your faith automatically increases and propels you to take a bigger risk. You should reward yourself for absolutely everything you do. Even small accomplishments should be rewarded. You have an internal reward system that if you don't reward yourself externally at times, will cause you to sabotage your efforts. When this happens, you can easily become discouraged which leads to diminished accomplishments or erode the things that you have worked so hard to accomplish in the first place. So reward yourself and do it often as you begin to see results for everything you do.

> *"Effort only fully releases its reward after a person refuses to quit."*
> – Napoleon Hill

I have a reward system built into my business, I literally do not do any personal shopping until I accomplish my goals. Here is what I do. I have a list of things that I need (not pressing), so I tag each item to a goal. That means if I don't achieve that goal; I am not having that particular need met.

In the second year of his business , James Cann, the British entrepreneur and TV personality said in his book 'Get the life you really want', that he sets himself the target of making a profit of £100,000 and actually made £400,000. So he got himself a silver bullet - Rolls Royce. Though the car seem over the top, but he said it had a massive impact on his motivation. Every time he got into the driving seat of the Rolls Royce, he believed, "if I carry on doing this, I can realise more of my dreams."

You don't have to spend everything you have to reward yourself. Sometimes this could be as little as going out with friends, dinner with my spouse, buying a new bag, changing my ipad. Tagging these items with my goals has helped me achieve a lot within a short time frame and even more importantly, it makes me feel good about the things I do.

Remember, rewarding yourself does not have to relate to your business matters, it can also be personal development, education, business, family and a host of other avenues where you can link a reward to. You don't have any reason not to reward yourself and I believe that is the easiest thing to do. After all, you love yourself. Let the love for yourself motivate you to begin planning some rewards for things you want to accomplish. It is said that, those who reward themselves really do end up being some of the happiest people on planet earth. Just make sure to do it in a way that is congruent and healthy to your lifestyle.

Here are simple reward tips called: The James Caan approach

- A reward for reaching a milestone doesn't have to be expensive, but should mean something to you. It will have real value for you because it represents an achievement.
- If you wait too long before rewarding yourself, the journey can feel much longer than it needs to and you may never see the fruits of your labour.
- Each reward becomes another piece of motivation for what you want to achieve. It reminds you of how good you'll feel when you reach the next milestone.
- Recognise the importance of celebrating your success. It will help you to become consistently successful.

CHAPTER THIRTEEN

WHAT NEXT?

"There is a science of getting rich, and it is an exact science, like algebra or arithmetic. There are certain laws which govern the process of acquiring riches and once these laws are learned and obeyed by anyone, that person will get rich with mathematical certainty."
—Wallace D. Wattles

World changer, influential, extraordinary, are some of the words used to describe highly successful people. It is a remarkable achievement to be described as such although few people make it. When we hear or read about them, it often paints a picture of a perfect journey to success. It is like watching a romantic movie- Roses, chocolate and so on. What we don't consider is the number of heart breaks the people involved may have encountered. Many of these extraordinary people may have failed several times, their career or business notwithstanding. What they have in common, however, is their persistent drive and large appetite for success. So much so, that when they encounter any setbacks, they are able to pick themselves up again. I have provided some examples in the book to show you that if you want to succeed you should expect a bit of failure along the way but take responsibility for it and understand that processing time comes before harvest.

Another issue is that when people talk about success, they narrow it to business only. The laws mentioned in this book are derived from universal laws using scientific methods of observation. Which means, whatever success you desire, be it in career, marriage, relationships or academics, these laws are applicable to all areas of life.

Again, when you consider people who have applied these laws and demonstrated outstanding results and then you look at your own situation but can see little or no relevance, you should be aware that those factors which created success in one individual may not have been the ones which underpinned success in another. However, at a more basic level, they all tend to demonstrate similar attributes to those which I have selected in this book. One form of misapplication is the failure to recognise that you have to take a holistic view of the laws. Their real impact is in the underlying values and their holistic application, not in the parts. It is not supposed to be applied via detailed steps, rather by reinforcing the theories into your daily activities so that they naturally become a way of life.

Those who have gained only an abstract understanding but not an in-depth knowledge, tend to misapply these laws. Therefore I recommend you gain personal knowledge through a dedicated commitment to understanding and holistically applying the laws to achieve results. Gaining this personal knowledge involves self-discovery that starts with understanding the underlying universal laws and their theories. It also requires seeing how the theories contribute to your longer-term vision and then repeatedly applying them over time. Once you understand these theories, you will be able to continually question your activities and be able to predict results, based on the law of cause and effect. You can only reap what you sow.

The process of self discovery requires personal knowledge and begins with a mindset that constantly seeks out gaps between where you are and where you want to be; what is and what could be. It is like walking through the jungle; your search will lead you to hunches, which, although they cannot be fully articulated, could drive you towards enlightenment. Once you are enlightened, your awareness increases which enables you to seek clarity.

This is the purpose of this book- 'The Next Maverick'. What I have provided in the book is a path to incremental improvements in your life irrespective of your career or future ambitions. It is to help you seek clarity.

The first step is to identify where you are across the twelve laws, then consider where you are most susceptible and then engage in some creative action planning sessions into how you can improve your situation. You might need to get some help. Perhaps this is where a Coach, Therapist, Spiritualist, Business Advisor or Mentors could help. Do not pressurise yourself to make changes at once or in a hurry.

Since the future is unknown, those contributing to shaping it and influencing it positively must be given every possible opportunity consistent with their performance and capabilities. At the most fundamental level, 'The Next Maverick' aims to encourage creativity for individuals, businesses and society at large: To quicken the reader to be aware of the laws highlighted and to apply them effectively for desirable results. If this book facilitates such creativity and its intended results, then it would have served its purpose.

REFERENCES

Allen. J, (2012), As a Man Thinketh: USA. CreateSpace Independent Publishing Platform

Blumenthal, K (2012) Steve Jobs: The Man Who Thought Different : Great Britain. Bloomsbury

Bonnke, R (1999), Faith: The link with God's Power: United kingdom, Sovereign World Ltd.

Branson, R (2006), Screw It, Let's Do It: Lessons In Life: United Kingdom. Virgin Books

Burg , B. and Mann, J.D., (2010), The Go-Giver: A Little Story About a Powerful Business Idea: Great Britain. Penguin

Caan , J (2012), Get the Life You Really Want: Quick Reads series; England. Penguin books

Cialdini, R, B. (2007) 'Influence: The Psychology of Persuasion,' Revised Ed. New York. HarperCollin.

Crossen, C (2001), The Rich & How They Got That Way: How the Wealthiest People of All Times - from Genghis Khan to Bill Gates - Made their Fortunes: Nicholas Brealey Publishing; Finland

Ericsson, K. A., Tesch-Romer, C, & Krampe, R. (1993). *The Role of Deliberate Practice in the Acquisition of Expert Performance* : Psychological Review; 1993, Vol. 100. No. 3, 363-406. American Psychological Association, Inc.

Gikandi, D.C (2008), A Happy Pocket Full of Money: Your Quantum Leap into the Understanding, Having, and Enjoying of Immense Wealth and Happiness: United States. Xlibris Corp

Gladwell, M. (2008), *Outliers: The Story of Success*. Great Britain. Little Brown and Company.
Hill, N (1937), Think and Grow Rich: Revised Ed., by Pell, A.R; Great Britain. Fawcett Publications

Jakes, T.D., (2000),The Great Investment: United States. G.P Putnam's & Sons.

Mair, G (2001), Oprah Winfroy: The Real Story; USA. Citadel Press

Mandela, N (1995), Long Walk To Freedom: The Autobiography of Nelson Mandela: Great Britain. New Ed ; Abacus.

McKaskill, T (2010), Venture Growth Strategies: A practical guide to engineer high growth into an entrepreneurial business: Australia. Breakthrough Publications

Osterwalder , A (2010), Business Model Generation: A Handbook for Visionaries, Game Changers, and Challengers; USA. John Wiley & Sons.

Roddick, A (2000), Business As Unusual: The Journey of Anita Roddick and The Body Shop. Great Britain. Thorsons.

Silbiger S (2001) The Jewish Phenomenon: Seven Keys to the Enduring Wealth of a People. USA. Longstreet Press

William, H. (2003). "The Man Who Lit Up the World".*TheFreeLibrary.com*. American Opinion

Websites:
Enelvolson, N: '(2012) Social Entrpreneur'
http://www.imasocialentrepreneur.com/category/social-entrepreneurs/
http://iempowerself.com/6_Body_energy_system.html
http://www.oprah.com/omagazine/Boost-Your-Self-Esteem-An-Interview-with-Nancy-Etcoff-PhD
History of Personal Computers: http://www.britannica.com/
Biographies: http://en.wikipedia.org/wiki/Portal:Biography
Johnson, B.D: http://wiredtogrow.com/
http://creativeoverflow.net/why-9-out-of-10-small-businesses-fail/
http://www.1888articles.com/
http://www.internationalpeaceandconflict.org/profiles/blogs/the-man-nelson-mandela-vision#.Ug3OO21FluO